MOTHER ANGELICA
HER GRAND SILENCE

MOTHER ANGELICA
HER GRAND SILENCE

The Last Years and
Living Legacy

RAYMOND ARROYO

IMAGE

NEW YORK

Library of Congress cataloging-in-publication data
is available upon request.

ISBN 978-0-7704-3724-4
eISBN 978-0-7704-3725-1

Printed in the United States of America

Book design by Lauren Dong
Jacket design by Jessica Bright
Jacket photography: (front) Our Lady of Angels Monastery;
(back) Raymond Arroyo

1   3   5   7   9   10   8   6   4   2

First Edition

In Memoriam

Mary M. Angello, loving grandmother and
one of the first to introduce me to Mother Angelica
1928–2013
and
Loretta Barrett, agent extraordinaire and the first
person in publishing to believe in Mother's story

Those whom I love I reprove and chasten;
so be zealous and repent.
Behold, I stand at the door and knock.

REVELATION 3:19–20

He who has the bride is the bridegroom. . . .
He must increase, but I must decrease.

JOHN 3:29–30

CONTENTS

INTRODUCTION

THE SPACIOUS CELL at the monastery where she spent her last years was almost always muggy—like any grandmother's room. The whir of the oxygen machine in the corner ricocheted off the tiled floor, providing the only constant sound in the space. Bookshelves and a dresser near her bed were laden with statues of saints, an oversized Child Jesus, religious cards, and relics. And there, bundled in a hospital bed, beneath a faded painting of the wounded Savior, a white ski cap atop her head, lay the most powerful and influential woman in Catholicism: the indomitable Mother Angelica.

As late as 2010, although she was bedridden and weakened by a stroke, the old nun's spunk remained intact. I walked into Mother's cell one afternoon to find her tugging the bedsheets up over her mouth, engaged in a daily war.

"Mother, you have to eat if you want to stay strong and healthy," the tiny Vietnamese nun, Sister Gabriel, fussed, extending a spoonful of mashed potatoes toward Mother's face. Angelica, having none of it, turned her glance toward the doorway.

"Is she trying to force-feed you again?" I jokingly asked as I entered.

Mother smiled broadly, tilting her face toward Sister Gabriel's spoon, and lowered the bed linen. Then just as the food approached, she yanked the sheet up again blocking the potatoes' entry.

"Oh, Mother," Sister Gabriel said in frustration. Delighting in the mayhem, Angelica let loose a wheezy cackle for my benefit. She winked at me and then having had her fun, quickly opened her mouth to accept the first morsel of lunch.

"She always gives me a hard time with lunch. Don't you, Mother?" Sister Gabriel said, offering a second scoop of potatoes. Mother pursed her lips and slowly shook her head from side to side. Lunch was over.

The moment struck me as classic Mother Angelica: the steely will, the slightly subversive humor, the joy that millions all over the globe had come to love were on full display for anyone entering that overheated room. I was partly to blame for the show. Sister Catherine, the onetime vicar of Our Lady of the Angels Monastery, claimed that Mother would "perform" when I showed up. It was as if she remembered the fun we had in days gone by and wanted to let me know that she was still game—her disability be damned.

My regular visits with Mother Mary Angelica never really ended. The frequency of our personal meetings was impeded by her stroke and her eventual confinement to the cell, but they continued—vastly altered—right up until her passing.

Mother Angelica hired me as news director at EWTN in 1996 and over time became much more than an employer to me. I cohosted her *Mother Angelica Live* program for a few years, and we often had long personal conversations at the end of the workday or after the live shows on Tuesday and Wednesday evenings. While I was working on her biography, from 1999 to 2001, we'd meet every Saturday in her monastery parlor, peering at each other through the wrought-iron latticework separating the world from the cloister. During those intense interviews she could be explosive, hilarious, conspiratorial, and holy—at times all at once. With Italianate gusto she shared how a tenacious faith reshaped the life of a wounded girl from Canton, Ohio, and changed the world.

In the lusterless suburbs of Birmingham, Alabama, this crippled nun, who barely graduated high school, founded a cable network in her cloister garage in 1981. She would tend the fledging operation for two decades, crossing swords with errant bishops, beating back takeover attempts, and struggling with her own infirmity to make the Eternal Word Television Network the largest religious media organization on the planet. It was her personality—her particular ability to connect with viewers and spiritually console them in moments of distress—that propelled the thing forward. They could feel her faith and were warmed by it. Away from the cameras, it was Mother Angelica's mystical intimacy with pain and suffering that fueled EWTN's growth and made her one of the world's most beloved spiritual figures.

The rigid white headgear of her habit could barely contain the nun's expressive face as she related the dramatic turns in her life during our times together. With each interview my understanding of her deepened along with our friendship. At times Mother would get so comfortable, especially over shared meals, that she would shift her weight in the overstuffed leather parlor chair, place a long, lean hand against her face, and really open up. She'd share troubles and fears, intimacies and secrets restricted to only a few of her sisters.

In June 2001 our conversation turned to some bishops who had caused her heartache in the past, men who never really cared for Mother's spiritual emphasis or style: "They don't pay me any attention. They're just waiting for me to die. But I won't! Ha ha." Her eyes twinkled with mischief; a satisfied smile spread across her face. Then she exhaled and suddenly the mood changed. "I talked to the Lord recently," she confided in a hush, "and I said I would like to stay until the worst is over—for the Church, for the community."

The Lord accepted her proposal. But I doubt if even Mother could foresee the consequences of her request.

Later that year, on Christmas Eve, a stroke precipitated by a cerebral hemorrhage nearly killed Angelica, depriving her of the speech that had built her broadcast empire. In 2004, an injury would shrink her world, physically restricting her to a corner bedroom at Our Lady of the Angels Monastery. To outsiders, and even to some of her closest collaborators, it would appear Mother Angelica's story was over. The old abbess became ill, was shut up in her room, and waited for God to come for her. But there is much more to the story—a story that has been hidden from the public until now.

In her protracted silence—for more than a decade—Mother Angelica would struggle for her soul, fight for her religious community, see the fulfillment of her last mission, and radically transform the lives of people she had never known. She would indeed stay until the worst was over.

Our society has a tendency to ignore or diminish the value of the infirm and the frail elderly. Their suffering and physical debilitation are reminders of our own mortality and the last act that awaits us all. But as the lives of Blessed Mother Teresa and Saint Pope John Paul II teach us, the end can be the most efficacious part of a life. It is a time of weakness and physical hardship, but it can also be one of spiritual union with God. For those striving for holiness, the "last things" can include supernatural attacks—temptations to doubt after a lifetime of belief. Mother was no exception. As I spoke to the sisters who cared for Mother, I learned details about her last years that even those closest to the monastery could not fathom.

In these pages are the particulars of Mother's 2004 secret journey to the Far East, a trip that would cost her dearly; firsthand, in-depth revelations of her physical struggles and the abiding faith that sustained her—even through the upheaval of her own religious community; accounts of the supernatural phenomena surrounding Mother in her last days and the spiritual warfare she waged in her cell; as well as intimate stories of her early years never before seen in print.

When I reviewed the three years of interviews I had conducted with Mother—her final interviews—I came across things I didn't know existed, or had overlooked as I was writing the biography. Mother's unpublished words shed new light on her painful final years, and put them in astonishing perspective. Having written an exhaustive biography of Mother Angelica and edited three volumes of her teachings and prayers, I thought I had written my last Mother Angelica book. My intention was to compose an epilogue for the biography consisting of a few details of her last days with some excerpts from our interviews and leave it at that. But when I sat down to write, so much new material emerged that another book presented itself.

Equally as fascinating as the facts surrounding Mother's last years are the many lives she influenced during her long public absence. Via reruns on EWTN,

Mother continued (and continues) to be a part of our lives. Though her live television career was long over, the heart of her ministry—pain and suffering offered up for the good of others—continued unimpeded in her final cloistered years. Gathered here is the fruit of her labors: the personal testimonies of many people scattered throughout the world whom she reached spiritually from a monastery bed in Hanceville, Alabama.

This work also permits me a chance to reflect on my personal relationship with Mother Angelica, something I have never written about before.

What follows is the conclusion of Mother's biography, a synopsis of her life leading up to this work, my personal account of our loving friendship, and a tribute to a cherished spiritual icon.

Attentive readers will notice that EWTN is mentioned only in passing here, as it had little connection to Mother in her final years. Following her resignation in 2000 and full withdrawal in 2001, she had no input into the day-to-day affairs of the network, nor was she or her sisters involved in the administration. That said, the spiritual ties to EWTN ran deep, and Mother always considered the network part of a personal mission entrusted to her alone.

LONG AGO, MOTHER made me promise to "tell the full story" of her life. This is the final chapter of that story—one that is as startling and inspiring as everything that preceded it. Reverend Mother, this is for you.

Even now, I still meet with Mother in memory and in spirit. And though I miss her physical presence, the writing of this work has allowed me to once again spend long hours with Reverend Mother and share her essence with others. This final book in the canon captures the last bittersweet years of a faithful woman who, in her grand silence and through great pain, transformed more lives and did more good than anyone could have imagined. It is also an opportunity to have one last visit with the sister we called "Mother."

Raymond Arroyo
Virginia, APRIL 2016

CHAPTER 1

The Last Journey

We need to suffer patiently not only the burden of being ill, but being ill with the particular illness that God wants for us, among the people that He wants us to be with, and with the discomforts that He permits us to experience.

—ST. FRANCIS DE SALES

THE OLD ABBESS had that familiar twinkle in her eye when I popped the question. Only one eye was visible at the time, as a black patch, secured by her glasses, covered the other. The left side of her face had been paralyzed by a series of ministrokes a few weeks earlier. The mouth that had so often held smiles now turned downward, distorting her speech. During what was to be our last formal interview, in November of 2001, I asked Mother Angelica what would be her next great work—her next project. She paused for a moment, brushed some cookie crumbs from her habit (since we were snacking at the time), and said in a slurred voice, "Foundations. The Lord is calling us now to give Him new foundations—new monasteries. We've got a lot of nuns here, and I think that's what we're supposed to do next."

At that point, Mother Angelica was in the midst of a long-desired, if rather ambitious, retirement. For a contemplative Poor Clare nun, Angelica was always a doer and a builder, a foundress of not only a couple of religious orders, but of a massive international broadcast empire. In March of 2000 she had retired from the Eternal Word Television Network; and though she would continue to host the *Mother Angelica Live* show, her goals had changed. As she entered her seventy-eighth year, the abbess intended to spend her retirement in the cloister, meditating on the Scriptures, mothering her community, and eventually sending nuns out to build new monasteries.

Those plans evaporated on Christmas Eve of 2001. That day a devastating stroke caused by a brain hemorrhage nearly killed her. In the aftermath, Mother's speech was severely restricted, her movement limited. She was forced to focus on her physical recovery. Even pushing a walker through the monastery hallways proved challenging. Suddenly reading her beloved Scriptures became a chore. She could no longer find the words to teach lessons to her nuns, and the hope of overseeing the construction of new contemplative houses seemed beyond reach.

Long before the stroke, some of her sisters—junior professed nuns in the late 1990s—remember Mother giving them lessons in the cramped Birmingham monastery that was once their community home. In their recollection she would scan the faces of her young daughters and, on more than one occasion, announce, "Prepare, sisters, the Lord will scatter you like rose pedals across the land." Her young sisters would not soon forget the prophetic summons.

In 2004, a plump, bouncy nun, Sister Mary Fidelis, scurried through the halls of Our Lady of the Angels seeking her friend, Sister Marie Andre. Fidelis felt God was calling her to continue her religious life elsewhere. She had heard that a bishop out west was looking for contemplative nuns to reside in his diocese. In an attempt to discover if anyone shared her wandering spirit, Fidelis cornered Marie Andre: a slender nun with crescent-shaped eyes who had an adventurous spirit and a fondness for the Lord of the Rings trilogy. When asked if she had any interest in leaving the Shire of Hanceville to begin a new foundation, Sister Marie Andre refused. But later, in June of that year, after being diagnosed with breast cancer, Marie Andre had a change of heart.

"I had a strong sense that the Lord was calling me to found a new foundation," Sister Marie Andre told me. "You would have thought that I would have wanted to stay put, since I was going through chemo. But I believe the Lord wanted to take me out of my comfort zone."

Sisters Marie Andre and Fidelis shared their thoughts with the vicar of Our Lady of the Angels Monastery, Sister Mary Catherine. Catherine was Mother Angelica's right-hand nun, the second in command, who oversaw the day-to-day affairs of the monastery during Mother's health woes. The vicar was a practical but impulsive nun from Louisiana's bayou country. Once informed that these young sisters felt God calling them to create a new foundation, possibly in Phoenix, Arizona, she leapt into action. In the late summer of 2004, the vicar and the two younger nuns presented the idea to Mother Angelica.

The old abbess was resting in her room when they appeared. The nuns explained what they had discerned, told Mother that the bishop of Phoenix would welcome contemplatives into his diocese, and asked her permission to found a new monastery. Mother listened intently, eyed Sisters Marie Andre and Fidelis, then deliberately declared, "I say, go!" The sisters quickly wrote Rome for permission.

News that younger sisters were initiating a new foundation was not viewed happily by a select group of the forty-two nuns residing at Our Lady of the Angels Monastery. Some of the senior professed nuns thought there should be no new foundations since their current home, which cost tens of millions of dollars, was barely five years old. There were also hard feelings about the way these younger nuns had proceeded without first securing the blessing of the senior sisters at a chapter meeting. With the full support of their vicar, Sister Catherine, the young nuns had rearranged the order of the necessary permissions. They would eventually seek the blessing of the professed nuns. But not initially.

It was all reminiscent of the way another superior, Mother Veronica in Canton, Ohio, had enabled the vision of one of her young nuns—a certain Sister Mary Angelica—to become a reality in the late 1950s. The abbess was a huge booster of Sister Angelica's dream to build a monastery in the South, with the goal of praying for racial healing. The announcement that Angelica was making plans to erect a Birmingham foundation set off intense rivalries within the walls of Sancta Clara Monastery in Canton. In the end, Angelica secured the needed permissions, and her abbess allowed her to take some of the monastery's best young sisters to the South. The superior's actions would deprive the Canton monastery of future leaders and destabilize it for years to come.

Perhaps the memory of all this caused the older nuns at Our Lady of the Angels Monastery to hesitate when talk of a new foundation surfaced in 2004.

There was a nucleus of nuns who regularly congregated in Mother Angelica's cell. This small cadre of sisters was part of a long-standing inner circle that surrounded Mother long before she took ill. Each served her abbess in a unique way, and each is at least partially responsible for the longevity Mother enjoyed in the wake of crushing physical limitations. They sometimes referred to themselves as "Little Mothers":

Sister Margaret Mary, the nurse: a solemn nun of delicate constitution and refined tastes. She was the dispenser of medicines, the final word on Mother's health, and the shadow designer of the Shrine of the Most Blessed Sacrament in Hanceville.

Sister Michael, the cook: a loyal sister of Polish descent with a reedy voice and definite opinions. She was one of the original nuns who traveled from Ohio to Alabama with Mother Angelica in 1962.

Sister Regina, the gardener: a hearty Southern nun with an easy Italian laugh and a fierce devotion to her abbess.

Sister Gabriel, the laundress and caretaker: a diminutive Vietnamese firecracker of a sister. She doted on Mother, ensuring that her habit and bed things were always spotless right up to the end.

Sister Agnes, the secretary: a talkative sister who possessed both brains and beauty. She had a wry sense of humor and eyes on the back of her veil.

Sister Antoinette, the historian and violinist: a solid, bespectacled Italian with a love of community history and an obedient heart.

Some of these sisters harbored reservations about the new monastery proposed for Arizona. And they were not alone. The vicar, Sister Catherine, informed Sister Marie Andre that she was unsure whether a majority of professed nuns would ever sign off on the foundation. Hopes for the new monastery flagged.

On the morning of November 19, Sister Marie Andre had a vivid dream: "Mother was in her wheelchair outside the door of the chapel in Hanceville. She called me by my baptismal name and said, 'Meghan don't worry, the sisters will be okay. You will go. You will go.'" Despite the consolation, given all she was hearing, Marie Andre was certain the older sisters would never approve the Arizona foundation. After receiving her chemotherapy that morning, Marie Andre sent word to the officials in Phoenix that the new monastery "was not going to happen." Later that afternoon, Sister Catherine unexpectedly called a chapter meeting.

The solemn professed nuns assembled, including the ailing abbess in her wheelchair. Sisters Marie Andre and Fidelis attempted to make the case that they were merely doing what Mother Angelica had done when she left Canton, Ohio, to start a new foundation in Alabama.

"You can't compare yourself to Mother," one of the older nuns said, correcting them. Angelica struggled to speak. The aphasia had so diminished her powers of expression. She could hear the words she wished to speak in her head, but her lips failed to produce them accurately. After some time she was able to convey something about the foundation being "God's will." A vote was taken, and the foundation in Phoenix surprisingly gained approval by the chapter. Sister Marie Andre and four other nuns quickly turned their attention to the West, beyond the walls of Our Lady of the Angels Monastery. At the same time another group of sisters turned to the East—the Far East.

Foundation Fever

MOTHER ANGELICA'S CELL was not only where the abbess slept, but a meeting room for those sisters closest to her. Here the nuns in the inner circle would regularly discuss monastery business, share information with Mother, or just recreate around old episodes of *I Love Lucy*. By 2004, the sisters would rotate, taking turns in Mother's room so every nun had a chance to get to know her abbess. But there were some sisters who were regulars in the room by virtue of the service they provided to Mother. Sister Margaret Mary was one of those sisters. She was Angelica's constant caretaker and ensured that the visiting nuns properly attended to Mother. So it only stood to reason that when Sister Antoinette had something to share with Margaret Mary, she would go to Mother's room to do it. Such was the case in late 2004, around the same time that word was spreading about the Phoenix monastery.

For some time Sister Antoinette, the community historian, had been corresponding with a member of their order in Japan. Though she had never met Sister Agatha of the Fukuoka monastery, Sister Antoinette was well aware of the Japanese nun's plight. Sister Agatha hoped to reestablish the monastery in Japan (where she resided) as a formal cloister. There was but one problem: Sister Agatha was the sole nun in the building.

When Antoinette shared the plight of the Japanese nun and her request for sisters, Margaret Mary felt inspired. Soon she was very enthused about starting a new foundation in Japan. In Mother's room the nuns excitedly began to plan a trip to Fukuoka to scout out the monastery. Sister Margaret Mary was going to be abbess of the new foundation, and Antoinette agreed to be her vicar. Their plan was to book a flight on Northwest Airlines for just the two of them. But Mother Angelica was listening.

Mother frowned, according to Sister Antoinette, each time the sisters discussed another exciting aspect of the Japanese voyage. Then, quite suddenly, the abbess announced that she "wanted to go." Angelica wished to be an active part of the adventure. And somewhere in the recesses of her injured brain perhaps she remembered: *Foundations. The Lord is calling us now to give Him new foundations—new monasteries.* The two sisters tried to talk Mother out of making such an arduous trip to the other side of the world. But the abbess had made up her mind. She was going to Japan to found a new monastery.

Realizing that resistance was futile, Sister Margaret Mary called a benefactor to arrange for a private plane; because of Mother's condition, commercial air travel was ruled out. Given Angelica's fragile health and limited mobility, Margaret Mary thought a doctor should join them. Two physicians, Michael Hall and James Hoover, did split shift, each taking one week in Japan. Father Joseph and Father Dominic of the Franciscan Missionaries of the Eternal Word, the male religious community Mother had founded, also agreed to make the trip. Margaret Mary purchased a set of Rosetta Stone CDs, which she and Mother used to begin learning Japanese in earnest.

On December 3, 2004, Mother Angelica, wearing her full habit and draped in a brown cape to fend off the cold, posed for pictures with the entire entourage on the tarmac in Birmingham. Sisters Gabriel, Michael, Antoinette, Margaret Mary, and the young sister Francesca could barely contain their excitement. Within moments, a couple of security guards who were also part of the traveling party strapped Mother to a metal chair and hoisted her into the private jet, ready for the 7,246-mile trip to Fukuoka, Japan. Not counting the refueling time in Anchorage, the flight would take fifteen hours.

Mother Angelica was eager to begin the last great journey of her life. Daunting, daring adventures were nothing new to the old nun. Difficult passages and trials, unexpected turns, and amazing graces had long marked her days. It had been so from the very beginning.

Rita Rizzo to Mother Angelica: 1923–2004

MOTHER ANGELICA'S JOURNEY started on April 20, 1923, in the red-light district of Southeast Canton. It was there that Rita Rizzo, a chubby child with a full head of dark hair, was born to what could politely be called a dysfunctional family. Her father, John, was a tailor and a well-practiced lothario. Her mother, Mae, was an elegant woman with the gift of gab who envisioned herself far away from the Italian slum where she had been born and raised.

On the day Rita was baptized, her mother placed the child on the altar of Our Lady of Sorrows. Looking up at the image of the mournful Madonna, swords thrust through her heart, Mae said, "I give you my daughter." From that day forward the child's dance with suffering and faith would be intense—and yield more beneficial results than even she could appreciate.

John had physically and verbally abused Mae long before Rita's arrival. By the time the child was five, her father abandoned the family and would not return for two years. Mae and Rita were left to fend for themselves. For a time they lived at Mae's family home on Liberty Street, but family squabbles and Mae's pride drove the mother and daughter to live in temporary housing and launch a series of laundry businesses that went nowhere. Little Rita grew up fast. As the girl struggled to make sense of why her father had abandoned her, Mae's emotional state deteriorated.

Rita bore a double burden: anxiety over her own well-being and deep concerns about the stability of the only parent she knew.

Shortly after John Rizzo resurfaced in town, Mae filed for divorce, on September 24, 1930.

Mother Angelica once shared a memory from this period that conveys her state of mind as a seven-year-old. Due to space limitations, I did not include this story in my biography *Mother Angelica: The Remarkable Story of a Nun, Her Nerve, and a Network of Miracles.*

On March 10, 1931, Rita's grandfather Anthony, dressed in a suit and vest, sought the child in the kitchen of the family home. He placed his hands on Rita's rounded shoulders. She stared up at the old man, her eyes like two black marbles, her mouth a tight slit—as if she was holding her breath.

"Rita, we're going to the courthouse," her grandfather said gravely. "You pray that the judge lets your mother keep you." Anthony patted her on the head, and then he, his wife, Mary, and Mae vacated the house.

"Well, I was petrified. I didn't know my dad that well. I hid behind the icebox, because I didn't know where else to go." Relaying the story to me decades later, Mother Angelica sounded like a frightened child. "When my grandparents and my mother came home, they were calling for me, and I wasn't going to answer. So my grandfather says, 'Rita, Rita, where are you?' No answer. Finally he must have caught on, so he says, 'The judge says your mother can keep you.' Well, I shot out from behind that icebox into my mother's arms. And that's when hell began."

Mae Rizzo spiraled into depression. Even three years after the divorce, she could not let go of John Rizzo. Mother Angelica told me how the mere sight of her father with another woman could send Mae into a rage: "We were at Lake Meyers with a friend. We were walking on the boardwalk, and Daddy came along with this woman. Well, [my mother] went bananas. I was crying, and it was just one horrifying experience. When we got home she got a horse rope: big and thick, braided and rough. She carried that rope in her purse for over a year. She said if she ever saw him again with anybody, she would let him have it. I remember anytime we went downtown I was petrified, absolutely petrified, because I knew what would happen if we saw him."

Mae started to talk of suicide and began having emotional breakdowns in front of her daughter. The unstable home life, her isolation at school, and her poor grades caused Rita to develop abdominal problems. She would get nauseous and double over in pain throughout the day, rarely eating without discomfort. By the age of eighteen, Rita had lost twenty pounds, necessitating medical attention. Doctors diagnosed her as suffering from ptosis of the stomach and prescribed a medical corset to relieve the pain. But her condition did not improve.

At that time a pattern emerged that would persist

throughout Rita Rizzo's life. In her darkest moments, when every option seemed exhausted and all hope lost, God would break through. On this occasion His instrument would be a housekeeper, Catherine Barthel, riding a bus home from work. Climbing aboard that same bus on January 8, 1943, Mae Rizzo spotted her old friend, Catherine. Mae chatted about Rita's situation and fretted that her daughter might never recover from her stomach ailment. Barthel offered an idea: "Why don't you take Rita to see Mrs. Wise?"

Rhoda Wise was a portly mystic in northeast Canton whose home Barthel regularly cleaned. Wise had personally experienced a painful intimacy with God. Throughout the 1930s she had endured repeated abdominal surgeries leaving her with a stinging wound on her abdomen and a ruptured bowel. In 1939, Wise converted to the Catholic Church. In agony, she prayed a novena to St. Thérèse of the Child Jesus for a healing. Months later Wise claimed that St. Thérèse, accompanied by Jesus, appeared at her bedside. The saint laid a hand on Wise's abdomen and healed her open sores. By Good Friday of 1942, Wise bled from her head, hands, and feet—suffering the wounds of Jesus. News of her stigmata and healing powers spread, drawing hundreds to her small house each week.

Rita and Mae raced to Wise's door, seeking God's intercession like so many before them. Rhoda Wise did not lay hands on Rita; she merely instructed the young

woman to pray a novena to St. Thérèse and gave her a
prayer card. Rita prayed the novena for a healing and
waited. Her faith was hardly active at the time.

Though Rita's family went to church on certain
holidays, Mother told me her religious instruction was
largely confined to observing the pieties of her grandparents. Whenever Rita and her grandfather passed a
Catholic church, he would pause for a moment, tip his
hat, and offer a salute.

"Grandpa, what are you doing?" Rita would ask, observing the strange ritual as a child.

"You wouldn't understand," the old man would say in
his singsong English. "When I pass the church I take
my hat off to Mary and to salute the Lord." The memory of this simple act would live with Rita well into old
age, teaching her the importance of an expressive faith.
Rhoda Wise taught her the power of faith—and the
meaning of redemptive suffering.

Nine days after she started her novena, Rita's stomach pain dissolved and she fell in love with Jesus. It was
a passionate love affair.

"When the Lord came in and healed me through the
Little Flower, I had a whole different attitude. I knew
there was a God; I knew that God knew me and loved
me and was interested in me. I didn't know that before,"
Mother said. "All I wanted to do after my healing was
to give myself to Jesus." Pious devotions became part of
her daily routine and spiritual literature her obsession.

Rita volunteered at Rhoda Wise's house, literally sitting at the bleeding foot of the suffering mystic.

When the Beloved called, nineteen months later, Rita responded. Feeling the tug of religious life, she visited several monasteries, finally settling on the Franciscan Nuns of the Most Blessed Sacrament, a Poor Clare order in Cleveland, Ohio. Knowing that Mae would never give her blessing to the idea of Rita entering a cloistered community, the girl jumped on a bus and sent her mother a special-delivery letter to announce her relocation. It would be a wrenching separation for both Rita and Mae. In time, not only would her mother come to peace with the decision, but years later Mae became a nun herself and joined Angelica's religious community in Birmingham.

Monastic life was an adjustment for Rita, who was now reborn as Sister Mary Angelica of the Annunciation. The outgoing nun immersed herself in Catholic classics by St. Teresa of Avila, St. John of the Cross, and Brother Bernard of the Resurrection. These works would profoundly shape her worldview and the ministry that was to come. All the while, physical maladies plagued Sister Angelica—notably a pair of knees that swelled whenever she climbed the stairs of St. Paul's Shrine. The knees became such an obstacle to her vocation that in 1946, as a last resort, her superiors sent her to a new monastery the order was founding in her hometown of Canton. Sancta Clara, the new convent, was a former mansion with fewer flights of stairs. Angelica's knees responded well, swiftly decreasing in size while her activity increased.

She was "into everything," according to Sister Michael, who met Mother at Sancta Clara. If there was a busted pipe, a loose cabinet, or a grotto to be built, Angelica was on the scene. She became the monastery contractor, one capable of guilting "the boys" from the old neighborhood—collectively called "Angelica's Tonys" by the other nuns—into donating their time and labor to her projects.

By 1952, Angelica had the notion of starting a new foundation dedicated to praying for racial healing. She imagined it would attract black nuns to the religious life. This was a natural aspiration for Sister Angelica, who had grown up in an integrated neighborhood in southeast Canton. She was sensitive to racial discrimination, and her mother, Mae, had a number of black friends. Sancta Clara also regularly hosted Inter-racial Days on the monastery grounds. But there would be no real movement on the new foundation until pain and Divine Providence showed Sister Angelica the way.

The thirty-year-old nun was cleaning a floor on the second level of her monastery in 1953 when the electric scrubber flew out of control, knocking her to the ground. The incident irritated a spinal defect, making it difficult for Angelica to straighten up. She resorted to traction, a brace, and finally surgery to relieve the pain. The night before a spinal fusion on July 31, 1956, her doctor was uncertain whether she would ever walk again. It was then that Angelica made an outrageous deal with God: "Lord, if you let me walk again, I'll build you a monastery in the South."

With great effort she did walk again, relying on crutches and a back and leg brace—leading her to comment years later, "When you make a deal with God, be very specific."

Pain had clarified her mission. The physical weakness it brought forced her to rely on God all the more. Angelica's letter to the bishop of Mobile, Alabama, in January of 1957 could not have been more specific. In it she wrote:

"Our great desire is to be in the midst of the colored people to intercede for them; we understand this mission would be more or less secret in order to prevent race difficulties; but we would like to be there for the colored, and in time . . . would hope even to have colored applicants for our community."

Bishop Thomas Toolin warmly welcomed the foundation, inviting Mother Angelica and her sisters into his diocese. It would take Angelica several more years to secure her local bishop's permission to proceed. But she was relentless. She had everything planned: sketches for the design, the sisters who would accompany her— she even started a fishing lure business to fund the new monastery. The sisters made the lures by hand and sold them via a newsletter. Her "St. Peter's Fishing Lures" soon turned a profit and demonstrated the nun's uncanny entrepreneurial prowess.

Our Lady of the Angels Monastery was formally established in Birmingham on May 20, 1962. During construction, Mother gave talks around town and became a beloved local figure. Though the initial inspiration for the monastery—to attract black contemplatives and pray for racial healing—did not pan out, Mother's lessons from that period reflected her enduring concern. She taught her nuns: "We can't say we love black people if we get up and move when they sit next to us, or if we don't want them in our schools."

The pressing challenge by 1967 was sustenance. Fishing lures did not seem to have the same appeal down south as they did in the north, so Mother shuttered the business. She tried growing strawberries and had the nuns stuff envelopes, but nothing worked. When a neighbor gave her the idea of roasting peanuts as a business, inspiration struck. Whether it was a peanut operation, a television network, a radio enterprise, or a foundation in Japan, when Mother Angelica felt inspired by God, there was no stopping her. She threw herself and everyone within reach into motion, seeking to accomplish God's will at any cost. The Lil' Ole Peanut Company was born in a matter of days. They sold the roasted treats to grocery stores, stadiums, bars, and schools, and retired the monastery debt a year later.

In the early 1970s Mother Angelica was swept up in
the charismatic renewal. An intense encounter with
"the Spirit," including the gift of speaking in tongues,
stimulated Mother's interest in the Scriptures. For the
first time, she began studying the Bible intensely. At the
urging of her bishop, Angelica agreed to give talks in Birmingham. She also consented to teach a Bible study to
a local women's Episcopal prayer group, but only during
Lent. When Lent ended, the women wished to continue
their lessons, so Mother invited them to her monastery
for a weekly Scripture study. It was during these meetings that Angelica refined her homespun approach to
the Gospels, vividly bringing the Good News to life
while mining the stories for practical spiritual guidance.
The Scripture conferences lasted for four years. At times
some of the regulars couldn't attend the meetings. Not
wanting to miss the abbess's teaching, they purchased
a tape recorder—thrusting Mother Angelica into her
next journey. She called the taped Bible lessons—which
eventually aired on local radio—*Journey into Scripture*.
Her message was straightforward and applicable to the
lives of those listening:

> We can become saints not because of what we
> are but because of what He is, and what He can
> make of us. Love is the one thing necessary. You
> must love God with your whole mind, your whole
> heart, with all your strength. He must be your all.

Let Him become part of your work and play . . . let Him be your constant companion throughout the day, speaking to Him as you would a friend.

Mother soon dissolved the Lil' Ole Peanut Company. She and the sisters were now running a media business. Using a secondhand dubbing machine, they made copies of Mother Angelica's talks and sold them for a dollar apiece. Mother would go on to compose a series of minibooks on the spiritual life. The extended pamphlets were written by hand in the monastery chapel on yellow legal pads. Each book offered Mother's unique advice about everything from suffering to prayer, to the Mass and the sacraments. An ever-growing audience seemed captivated by the spunky nun's message. The books led to invitations to speak across the country. One of these speaking engagements, in March 1978, would change her life and the Church forever.

It happened in a small Chicago TV studio, at the top of a skyscraper, where she had arrived for an interview. Seeing the broadcast lights, the small set, the cameras, Angelica muttered a quiet prayer, "Lord, I gotta have one of these." She had seen her future and this was it. "Boy, it don't take much to reach the masses, you know," Mother told those joining her in that Chicago studio. She could speak for a year straight, write hundreds of books, and never reach the audience that she could reach on television.

"My attitude is, if the Lord inspires me to do something, I attempt to do it," Mother explained to me. "I start and it goes like a snowball downhill. I have to start. If it's not His will, it will either fall apart or something will happen to really hinder it."

So she started. Mother turned to her friend Jean Morris, a willowy member of the Episcopal prayer group. Jean was tasked to find a studio, organize a television crew, and, by default, finance the venture.

After several attempts, the camera captured Mother's way with the Scriptures, her practical wisdom, and her irrepressible humor. In time, she had a reel to show broadcasters. The Christian Broadcasting Network was so taken with Mother's zeal and her ease before the camera, they ordered sixty episodes and gave her two months to shoot them. Angelica scrambled for funding while recording the series. She even returned to the speaking circuit, announcing for the first time in July of 1978 that the Catholic Church needed a satellite to beam the teachings of the Church to the masses.

During the recording of her second series, *In His Sandals,* Mother became aware of a forthcoming CBS miniseries entitled *The Word.* The plot concerned newly discovered ancient scrolls that challenged the divinity of Jesus. Mother was not exactly enchanted by the story line. In fact she considered it blasphemous. When Angelica realized that the station where she had been shooting her series was the local Birmingham CBS affiliate, she asked to see the general manager. Once the manager showed himself, the nun demanded that he refuse to air *The Word*. He rejected her request.

"I will not put my programs on this station, nor make any other programs here if you run that movie," Mother threatened. For her this was not just a movie, but an assault upon her Spouse, the Love of her life.

The station manager told her, "You leave here, you're off television. You need us."

"No I don't. I only need God. I'll buy my own cameras and build my own studio," she fumed.

After storming out of the studio, Mother returned to the cloister certain that she had ruined her broadcast ministry. To lift her spirits, the nuns suggested that she adapt what was intended to be a garage behind the monastery into a studio. Angelica instantly embraced the idea—and a media empire was born.

She began the great temporal work of her life with only two hundred dollars in the bank, scant knowledge, and nothing but faith to sustain her. Her radical belief would make all the difference. As she never tired of saying: "Unless you are willing to do the ridiculous, God will not do the miraculous. When you have God, you don't have to know everything about it; you just do it."

She would call her foray into cable the Eternal Word Television Network as a sly protest against *The Word*, the "blasphemous" miniseries that first moved her to action.

It was the funds she raised from her talks that sustained the fledgling operation in early 1981. So when her local bishop, Joseph Vath, suddenly forbade her to speak in public and the papal representative in Washington agreed, Mother was faced with a major crisis. With no other source of income, she dispatched her in-house lawyer, Bill Steltemeier, to New York to try to convince a visiting Vatican cardinal to come to EWTN. Steltemeier's mission was successful, and Cardinal Silvio Oddi of the Sacred Congregation for the Clergy soon arrived in Birmingham. The cardinal was so impressed by the fifty-eight-year-old nun's efforts that he promised to secure the exemptions from Church law for Angelica to continue her public speaking. On August 15, 1981, she threw a switch in the tight Birmingham control room and brought into being America's first Catholic cable channel. No other religious or layperson had ever attempted such an undertaking.

As she started EWTN, Mother's concern over the excesses of the charismatic movement deepened. Her friend Jean Morris recently shared a story that demonstrates Mother's perspective at the time. Jean and Mother were at lunch with a woman who was extolling the virtues of full-immersion baptism for adults—even if an individual had been baptized as an infant.

"But you don't need to do that—you've already been baptized," Angelica insisted. "The woman kept at it. But Mother stood her ground," Morris remembered. "Finally,

Mother dipped her finger in a water glass and flicked it in the woman's face, saying, 'There. Now you've been baptized twice.'"

Whatever her reservations about the charismatic movement, its effects could be felt in her speeches and television broadcasts. Mother had an allure and a passionate spark on television that no one in the Catholic Church at that time or since could match. There was a secret to her success. "A spiritual growth network must be rooted in the contemplative life," she told me. "I think this is why we were chosen. This is the most unlikely thing for a religious order, but God likes to do big things with little things."

In 1983, He did another big thing when Mother launched what would become the cornerstone of EWTN's programming: *Mother Angelica Live.* It was her chance to connect directly with the viewers in real time. The show afforded her a chance to reach people in their spiritual despair, in their depression, in their confusion and addictions and remind them that God was present. Humor became her greatest lure. People would flip on EWTN and start laughing. The nun was funny. Viewers found themselves fascinated by her delivery, her street lingo, her indescribable joy—her authenticity. They wanted what she had.

As a broadcaster, Mother Angelica was one of the few religious figures who acknowledged the mess everyday people encountered in their own lives: the annoyances, the disappointments, the miseries and setbacks. She didn't gloss over the contradictions we all experience; she embraced them and helped people find God in them.

Later Angelica renewed her activist tendencies, using her channel to defend her traditional beliefs. I have often said that Mother Angelica single-handedly saved the Church in America, and maybe around the world. When there were liturgical abuses, when devotions were being cast aside or disparaged, it was Mother Angelica who challenged the status quo and vigorously defended Church teaching. Then she took it a step further. Through her broadcast Masses, the rosary, chaplets, and prayers aired throughout the day, she showed the world how Catholicism was supposed to look. When a bishop or even a cardinal strayed from orthodoxy, Mother fearlessly called him out and offered humble corrections. Since I have catalogued so many of these instances in *Mother Angelica: The Remarkable Story of a Nun, Her Nerve, and a Network of Miracles,* I will refrain from resurrecting them here.

Mother's most impassioned on-air moments were reserved for those occasions when she felt her Spouse was being belittled or attacked in the public square. The release of Martin Scorsese's *The Last Temptation of Christ* in 1988 illustrates the point.

Shortly before the film's premiere, Mother received a scene-by-scene summary of the film's script. The movie depicted a deeply confused Jesus: a man who earned his

money making crosses for the Roman legion while fanta-
sizing about having sex with Mary Magdalene and raising a family with Mary and Martha. The film sparked a
torrent of Christian protest, primarily from evangelical
groups. And though the National Conference of Catholic Bishops found the film "morally objectionable," the
Catholic response was muted until Mother got involved.
The abbess hastily waged an on-air campaign to stop
the film, or at least to discourage people from viewing
it. She produced and aired a daily ten-minute report
on the movie. She wrote to President Ronald Reagan,
governors, and mayors, pleading with them to join the
boycott of the film. During her live show she rallied her
viewers to write letters of protest to Universal, the film's
distributor.

"I have compassion for prostitutes and drug ad-
dicts," she explained to her audience. "But I have no
compassion—I have absolutely no compassion—for
blasphemers who ridicule the Lord Jesus with these terrible movies . . . You belong to the EWTN family. I ask
you to revolt against this movie, and let them know that
this country is still under God." She ended with a de-
fiant challenge: "They're treating the Lord Jesus like a
dog. And you're going to sit there and do nothing? Well
I'm not! You can do what you want to do—I'm going to
holler. I'm going to yell and scream until something is
done."

Two weeks later she did just that when she appeared

on *Larry King Live*. With one arm thrown over the back of a swivel chair, as if she owned the place, Mother got in the face of her opponent, Jack Valenti, president of the Motion Picture Association of America. For the first time, Mother Angelica the street fighter emerged. She dominated the conversation from the outset, drolly calling both King and Valenti "sweetheart." Shoving an index finger in their faces, she asserted that no one had a right to "be entertained by blasphemy." Valenti tried to argue that even if Mother didn't like it, the filmmakers were entitled to artistic expression. "Oh, get off it," Angelica parried. Then she asked a telling question. She wanted to know how Valenti would react if someone depicted his daughter as a prostitute on film. The question revealed why the nun so despised a movie she had never seen. Since her days in Canton, the person of Jesus had been present and real for Angelica—as real as Valenti's daughter. To view *The Last Temptation of Christ* as a fictional exploration of the Messiah's humanity (as Scorsese described it) was impossible for Mother. In her eyes, it was a slanderous depiction of her living, active Spouse. Period. She reacted the way any loyal Italian wife from Southeast Canton would have reacted: unreservedly and with great passion.

When it was over, *The Last Temptation of Christ* earned an anemic $8.2 million at the box office, barely returning its investment.

In the fall of 1988, Mother Angelica wanted to retire

from the network and devote more time to her community when she got a message during prayer. She believed God was calling her to "begin a shortwave radio network." With no further instruction and no clear path, she resumed her prayers. Weeks later, Angelica found a line from the book of Revelation: "And I saw another angel flying through the midst of heaven, having the eternal gospel, to preach unto them that sit upon the earth and over every nation and tribe and tongue and people."

Convinced that she was being called to preach the Gospel to the whole world, Mother thought, where else am I to do that, if not Italy? Within days, Mother Angelica, a few nuns, and Bill Steltemeier were jetting to Europe on yet another journey of inspiration.

By April of 1989, she had opened a monastery north of Rome, in Olgiata, to pray for the radio venture, but setbacks in Italy made it too costly to continue. A Dutch millionaire, Piet Dirksen, provided much of the cash to fund the radio project, which eventually moved to Alabama. With additional funding from Joseph Canizaro, a New Orleans real estate developer, Mother became owner of one of the only nongovernmental shortwave operations in the world, WEWN, in 1992.

But there was a severe personal cost for all this success. With each advance in her work, Angelica experienced a corresponding physical hardship. "That has always been the preparation that God seems to give me,"

Mother said about her pain during an interview. "It always seems to precede something that the Lord wants me to do."

The shadow of the cross was never far from Mother Angelica as she pursued God's will. While building the shortwave network she took a spill outside a department store and shattered her wrist. Two broken bones protruded through her flesh. Mother described it to me as "the worst physical pain" of her life. For months she would wear a metal appliance to reset the bones. Not one to waste suffering, she offered the pain up "for the continuation of God's blessing on the work He has given me to do." According to Mother, the pain kept her totally reliant on God—and responsive to his promptings.

This relationship between pain and Providence can be tracked throughout Angelica's life. There would be heart attacks, vertebra-crushing bouts of asthma, dire infections, recurring back problems, all of which Mother took in stride and used to propel the mission of the moment. She called it a "foundation of pain" God had laid in her life. "That's how God works," she would explain. "Sometimes it takes more than prayer . . . it takes great suffering."

In March of 1995, an asthmatic episode nearly stopped her breathing and almost ended her life. Some would have been tempted to view the episode as a punishment or a distressing setback. Mother accepted it as God's will, recovered, and, in its aftermath, came away with a new understanding of Christ's suffering. Only months later her network would go international, reaching Europe, Africa, and Central and South America.

To promote EWTN's new reach, Mother traveled to South America in the summer of 1996. As was her habit, she visited a local shrine, in this case one dedicated to the Divine Child Jesus in Bogotá, Colombia. Mother claims that as she looked up at the statue of the Child Jesus, the figurine spoke, ordering her to: "Build me a temple and I will help those who help you." She got right to work, expanding an existing plan for a new monastery and traversing the world to commission furnishings, statues, flooring, and windows for His "temple."

On January 28, 1998, the seventy-five-year-old nun slowly teetered on her crutches, navigating a series of hallways connecting the convent to EWTN, en route to her live show set. The stress of building a new monastery, overseeing the network, and fighting an ongoing public battle with Cardinal Roger Mahony of Los Angeles had drained Mother's strength. Months earlier she had made a passing comment on her show expressing displeasure with the cardinal's recent pastoral letter on the Eucharist. Mother didn't like the way Mahony's letter diluted the teaching on transubstantiation and, in her opinion, diminished the True Presence: the actual Body, Blood, Soul, and Divinity present in the consecrated host and wine of the altar. Her exact words were "the cardinal of California is teaching that it's bread and wine before the Eucharist and after the Eucharist. I'm afraid my obedience in that diocese would be absolutely zero—and I hope everybody else's in that diocese is zero."

Cardinal Mahony would complain far and wide that Mother had violated canon law and had whipped up dissent in his diocese. Letters soon began flying back and forth, and not a few of them to Rome. The possibility was even raised that Angelica should be denied the sacraments as a punishment for her comments. She carried the weight of this drama with her as she advanced down the halls she had traversed thousands of times before. It would be the last time she would walk them on crutches.

That night a peculiar Italian mystic arranged to meet Mother in her office after the live show. The woman claimed to have a message from the Virgin Mary: she was to pray a rosary with Mother Angelica. Leery of the mystic's intentions, Mother consented to join the woman for a quick prayer and nothing more. In the middle of the fourth decade of the rosary, Mother Angelica felt "a warmth in [her] ankles." The mystic instructed her to remove her crutches, which she did. For the first time in forty-two years the nun could walk without crutches or braces. Mother saw the healing as a boon for the faith of the viewers and employees of EWTN. It would also provide a much-needed jolt of energy and physical freedom to a nun with lots to do.

In 1998, Mother Angelica would bring Catholic radio into being across the United States. That year she offered

EWTN's radio programming free of charge to any group that bought an AM or FM station. This allowed local Catholic stations to start up all over the United States and freed them from the burden of financing expensive programming. When Mother offered her free service in 1998 there were 14 Catholic AM and FM stations on the air; as of this writing there are more than 200.

Mother Angelica's new monastery, Our Lady of the Angels and the Shrine of the Most Blessed Sacrament in Hanceville, Alabama, opened its doors in 1999 at a cost of nearly $60 million. There was enough room for the thirty-one nuns and space to spare. Just as she completed this milestone, while the storm clouds of the Mahony affair were still dissipating, Mother found herself in conflict with her local bishop, David Foley of Birmingham. He was disturbed by the community custom of celebrating the Mass facing east (with the priest's back to the congregation) and began raising questions about who owned and controlled EWTN. The bishop contended that Our Lady of the Angels Monastery owned the network, but the network maintained that it was a public, lay-run organization. Unsatisfied with that answer, Bishop Foley requested a Vatican investigation of Mother Angelica, her community, and, tangentially, the network.

The Vatican visitation was thorough and invasive. As it continued, suspicions abounded, as did the fear of an unbearable solution: the possible removal of Mother

Angelica as abbess and the appointment of an outsider as the community superior and head of EWTN. Some of those closest to Mother at the network sounded dire alarms. To stop what she was led to believe were looming threats against her religious order, she did the unthinkable. Mother Angelica elected to resign from EWTN in March of 2000 with the support and encouragement of Steltemeier and many of her vice presidents. The network she had labored so hard to birth, and had tended for two decades, was hers no more.

The stress of the ecclesial battles and the investigation very likely brought on the cerebral hemorrhage and deadly stroke that felled Mother Angelica on Christmas Eve, 2001. Emergency surgery and the prayers of her sisters were all that saved her. Given the oxygen deprivation she experienced, her recovery was, in the words of one doctor, "miraculous." With the help of a walker she moved about the monastery and resettled into community life.

It was clear that Mother wished to regain the energy of days gone by. So in October of 2003 she made what many of us thought would be her final international journey, to Lourdes, France. She traveled to the famed grotto and miraculous springs in search of a healing. What Mother found in the sea of pain all around her was the spiritual strength to embrace her suffering, and to appreciate its rich value beyond the awful frustrations of the moment.

A little more than a year later, even the sisters were surprised when it was announced that Mother would be heading to Japan at the age of eighty-one. She was single-minded in her desire to reach the Far East as quickly as possible with no hindrances.

On the flight to the Japanese island of Kyushu, the private jet touched down in Anchorage, Alaska, to refuel. Fathers Joseph and Dominic had hoped to step out of the plane during the refueling—just to say that they had stood on Alaskan soil. But on their way down the aisle to the front of the plane, they ran into an obstacle. Mother Angelica threw her arm across the aisle, blocking the priests' passage. "Ah-uh," Mother said, staring bullets at them.

The priests never did step foot in Alaska.

"She wanted no accidents or delays," Father Joseph said.

At least Mother would have no delays.

Ad Orientem

THE JAPANESE VISIT had everything going for it. The trip fortuitously fell on the 150th anniversary of the founding of Angelica's order, the Poor Clares of Perpetual Adoration; Mother was in great spirits; and a monastery in need of sisters awaited the habited throng on the island of Kyushu. With over forty sisters in the Hanceville monastery, the abbess had nuns to spare. Mother

Angelica, the priests, Sisters Margaret Mary, Michael, Antoinette, Gabriel, Francesca, the security guards, and a doctor landed in Fukuoka on December 4, 2004.

Their first order of business was to see the monastery. It was situated in a heavily trafficked business district in the city. High-rises surrounded the building, and sirens sounded day and night. Sister Agatha, a survivor of the atomic bombing of Nagasaki, had managed to maintain three hours of adoration before the Blessed Sacrament daily, with the assistance of lay volunteers. So it was with great excitement that she greeted her American sisters and welcomed them to the austere monastery.

Sister Agatha had been essentially using the building as a boardinghouse for women in the area. Eyeing the state of the structure, Mother Angelica could not have been less impressed. As part of her therapy following the stroke, a therapist had taught Angelica to sing the words she wished to communicate as a way of overcoming the aphasia that stifled her speech. Wheeled down the hallways of the monastery, Mother sang out, to the tune of "Let It Snow": "Tear it down, tear it down, tear it down." Thankfully, Sister Agatha was not within earshot at the time.

A visit with the bishop of Fukuoka was even more disappointing. The bishop felt that establishing a cloistered order dedicated to prayer before the Blessed Sacrament would never work in his diocese. The people of Japan, he thought, would just not be receptive to, or even understand, the nuns' mission. Mother Angelica grimaced, instantly relaying her displeasure. "Let's go to Nagasaki," she suggested. Moving their schedule up by two days, the entire party traveled north, following her direction.

Through Sister Agatha, a meeting was hastily arranged with Archbishop Joseph Mitsuaki Takami of Nagasaki to see if he would be receptive to inviting contemplatives into his archdiocese. The prelate warmly received the nuns, according to the sisters, and was "elated" by the prospect of establishing a cloistered monastery in Nagasaki. Enlivened by the possibility of a foundation there, the sisters toured the area, including the Shrine of the Twenty-Six Martyrs Memorial outside the city.

At the hotel that evening, despite doctors' orders, Mother Angelica consumed a celebratory ice-cream sundae following dinner. Afterward, Sisters Margaret Mary and Antoinette and Mother reconvened upstairs to compose a formal letter to Archbishop Mitsuaki. The studious Antoinette was on the laptop computer, transcribing Margaret Mary's dictation. Mother nodded in approval as Sister Margaret Mary deliberately pronounced each line. The idea was to have Mother Angelica sign the letter when it was complete. But as they proceeded, Antoinette had a notion.

"Sister Margaret Mary has a very flowery, spiritual tone when she writes," Sister Antoinette said. "So I made the suggestion that Mother should write an introductory letter of her own and let Margaret Mary sign the one we were composing."

"Oh, so now we have two superiors?!" a miffed Mother

Angelica responded. Reverend Mother signed the only letter that was delivered to the archbishop before the nuns proceeded on to Akita, to visit yet another shrine.

Akita was the site of a Marian apparition—one that would have had particular resonance for Mother Angelica. In the summer of 1973, at a convent chapel just outside Akita, a nun, Sister Agnes Sasagawa, saw rays of light seeping from the tabernacle on the altar. More than a week later, "a cross-shaped wound" appeared on the palm of her left hand. It would bleed, bringing incredible pain to Sister Agnes. Then in July 1973, the nun thought she heard a voice emanating from a wooden statue of the Virgin Mary in the chapel. It spoke of the need to pray for the reparation of mankind's sins so as to avoid grave calamities and "a punishment greater than the deluge." That same day the nuns noticed that the right hand of the Marian statue was dripping blood. The three-foot carving of the Blessed Mother would bleed on several other occasions—and years later, it began to "weep."

Mother and the sisters were thrilled at the prospect of visiting the shrine at Akita. They flew into the city and boarded two vans to make the steep climb to the mountaintop shrine. Mother, seated in her wheelchair, was in the back of the second van. The uneven road was hard on the axle and caused a lot of bouncing for the travelers, but they finally made it to the top.

When one closely reads the three messages of Akita— which Sister Agnes believed were from the Mother of

God—the unlikely and providential visit of Mother Angelica to this remote shrine suddenly makes sense. In retrospect, the messages were almost a prefigurement of Mother's final journey, a foreshadowing of the difficult years that lay ahead.

On July 6, 1973, the Akita visionary was told to recite the prayer of the "Handmaids of the Eucharist" which includes these words: "Most Sacred Heart of Jesus, truly present in the Holy Eucharist, I consecrate my body and soul to be entirely one with Your Heart, being sacrificed at every instant on all the altars of the world . . . Please receive this humble offering of myself. Use me as You will for the glory of the Father and the salvation of souls."

Mother Angelica was lowered from the van and pushed into the large Japanese-style chapel. Inside, she was transfixed by the wooden statue of the Virgin Mary that had spoken to Sister Agnes thirty-one years earlier. The Virgin, who spiritually accepted unimaginable suffering, reached out not only to a Japanese nun, but to a particular ailing sister from Canton, Ohio.

"In order that the world might know His anger, the Heavenly Father is preparing to inflict a great chastisement on all mankind," the voice of the Virgin told Sister Agnes on August 3, 1973. "Many men in this world afflict the Lord. I desire souls to console Him, to soften the anger of the Heavenly Father. I wish, with my Son, for souls who will repair by their suffering and their poverty for the sinners and ingrates."

Mother Angelica and her nuns prayed for some time

before the wooden statue. They then proceeded to the gift shop, where they scooped up all manner of religious items. Angelica, with a faraway expression, watched her daughters dart about the store collecting their goodies.

The last message of the Blessed Mother in Akita spoke of "fire" falling "from the sky" that would "wipe out a great part of humanity." On October 13, 1973, she warned that "the work of the devil will infiltrate the Church . . . the demon will be especially implacable against souls consecrated to God. The thought of the loss of so many souls is the cause of my sadness." No wonder the statue wept on 101 separate occasions.

At the van, Mother Angelica sat in her rolling chair as the security guards situated her in the rear of the vehicle and fastened the wheels to the floorboard. The pocked road made the descent even more uncomfortable than the drive up. The travelers were repeatedly lifted off their seats and dropped with unnerving force. Mother's face pinched into a grimace from the jostling. In its aftermath, she closed her eyes, whispering, "Oh God. Oh God."

The flight back to America was a difficult one for Angelica. Each time her body was jostled, she yelped, as if in pain, her face contorted. During a mid-flight Mass, Father Joseph and several of the sisters recall Mother repeatedly moaning. She was clearly in some sort of physical agony, but no one could figure out exactly what ailed her. Later, watching a videotape of the midair Mass, Sister Gabriel became convinced she saw the Virgin Mary and Jesus "consoling" Mother Angelica during the flight.

Back at the monastery, Mother winced in pain even while in bed. She couldn't get comfortable and slept poorly. Sister Margaret Mary finally thought a doctor should be brought in to examine the abbess. His finding? Mother had fractured her tailbone, very likely during the descent from the shrine in Akita.

Please receive this humble offering of myself. Use me as You will for the glory of the Father and the salvation of souls. . . . the demon will be especially implacable against souls consecrated to God.

The injury made transferring Mother Angelica to the wheelchair all but impossible. The last thing left to her, her mobility, was now greatly diminished. The "foundation of pain" in Angelica's life had suddenly broadened, and a new source of sacrifice had opened to her. Mother's final prolonged journey had begun.

CHAPTER 2

The White Martyrdom of Mother Angelica

When you were young you girded yourself and walked where you would; but when you are old, you will stretch out your hands, and another will gird you and carry you where you do not wish to go.

—JOHN 21:18

AT CERTAIN TIMES of the day, the activity in the large cell at the end of the hallway of Our Lady of the Angels Monastery could have been mistaken for a nuns' martial arts demonstration. At prescribed hours, Sisters Michael, Margaret Mary, Gabriel, and others would physically battle their abbess in an effort to change her bed linens or clothing. And the struggle was not for the meek.

"She's strong," Sister Michael said of Mother Angelica at one point. "Those hands are very strong. And sometimes when she doesn't want to get up, those knees go flat and she will not budge." Faint bruises on Angelica's long skeletal hands testified to the fight still in her.

The Japan excursion marked a turning point in Mother's life. "That Japanese trip really did Mother in," Sister Grace Marie recalled in her proper English accent. "She was so much frailer when she got back from that trip."

In the wake of the Japan voyage, the abrupt loss of mobility and independence were difficult for Mother Angelica to bear. Of all the many crosses she willingly embraced throughout her long life—the crippled legs, the excruciating back pain, the endless ailments and illnesses, the inability to speak—this final cross would be the most onerous. In the past, despite her disabilities, she had been the superior, the CEO, the leader, the authority. Though she had lost the ability to communicate her thoughts, she still had limited mastery over her person. Now that was leaving her as well. Confined to her bedroom, under the watchful eyes of her sisters, she would by degrees surrender the last bit of her identity: the strong personality and the indomitable will.

Not long after her stroke, Mother told me the restricted speech and the physical limitations had a higher purpose. "Purification, my purification," she said without hesitating. Mother accepted the privations and recognized the spiritual value of her condition. But to release the last shred of control she still possessed— her self-rule—was an extreme sacrifice. For a fiercely independent woman to allow others to manipulate her person, to have food thrust upon her on a schedule not her own, was a type of horror that Mother initially resisted—at times ferociously.

"If Mother was going to show her will it was going to be with those who were caring for her," a sister regularly in the abbess's cell told me. "She would hit, grunt, make herself heavy as a board. She would refuse to turn over—fight me to change her bed. I would be just as stubborn with her, and use my strength to fight back. She would lock her joints and could do it for hours. She was very strong."

Part of Mother's resistance was attributable to the suddenness of these routines. She would wake from a deep sleep and straightaway someone was resituating her in bed or coming at her with a forkful of meatloaf. The deprivation of privacy and the loss of the silence she so cherished might have also contributed to her reticence.

Throughout early 2005, Angelica was rarely able to leave her room and was in excruciating pain. The fractured tailbone made it impossible to sleep on her back. Meals, baths, the dispensing of medications— everything now happened in the bed.

The nuns, led by Sister Margaret Mary, went into nursing mode, ensuring that Mother's every need was satisfied. Trimming her nails, washing her hair, preparing special foods—all aspects of Mother's daily life were overseen by the sisters with not only a sense of duty, but devoted affection. Many times I witnessed the thorough labors of the nuns, and the meticulous attention they brought to Mother's care. To them, time was no object, and failure no option. Despite her early resistance, Mother Angelica was deeply appreciative of their efforts. She would often stroke the sisters' faces or offer a spontaneous "I love you" after they finished a part of the daily regimen.

"She is very affectionate," Sister Mary Gabriel said. "Sometimes she'd give me hugs and kisses. It was hard for Mother. Ever since we got back from the Japan trip she could no longer get out of the bed as she had from time to time before."

Aside from the tailbone injury and the possibility of a new monastery in Nagasaki, the trip to Japan allowed Mother Angelica spiritual contact with one of Catholicism's two patron saints of missionary activity. The missionary saint Angelica was most familiar with, up to that point, was St. Thérèse of Lisieux. The French contemplative nun famously prayed for an unrepentant Parisian murderer, Henri Pranzini, in 1887. She offered Masses and sacrifices for the convicted man's conversion. Months later, Thérèse read that Pranzini, moments before his execution, had asked the chaplain for a crucifix to venerate as he prepared to enter eternity. From that moment on the nun dedicated herself to missionary work through prayer. It was through the intercession of St. Thérèse that Mother Angelica had been cured of a severe stomach ailment at nineteen—an event that paved the way for her religious vocation.

Then in the twilight of her long life, having spent decades praying for people she had never met and bringing a message of hope to the forgotten all over the world, Mother had crossed paths in Japan with the other great missionary saint, Francis Xavier. After evangelizing throughout India, Francis Xavier, a Jesuit, traveled through Japan establishing congregations on the islands there. Unlike so many of his Jesuit peers, he adapted his message to the local populace and often sought to convert the working classes.

Mother, in her final years, reflected the spirit of both these missionary saints. She would continue to pray and offer extreme sacrifices for humanity like Thérèse, while still burning with Francis Xavier's zeal to establish foundations in new lands. She would also encounter the same challenges, setbacks, and physical pain that her saintly predecessors had endured.

Departures and Divisions

THE STURDY SISTER ANTOINETTE poked her head around the door of Mother's room, a letter in hand. Wearing her bravest face, she nervously entered, unsure of the reception she might receive.

Since the return from Japan, whenever Antoinette entered the abbess's cell, Mother would lower her head, as if to avoid eye contact with the nun. The pattern of frosty greetings rattled the sister, who at the time had been a member of the community for eighteen years. Sensing the tension, Antoinette had a chat with Mother Angelica about the cool relations between them. During their conversation, Angelica managed to convey the message that Antoinette should not be part of the Japan foundation and, curiously, that she should leave the monastery in Hanceville—though not the order. Given Mother's difficulties communicating, Antoinette was left confused and distressed by these messages. The nun had been mulling her future at the monastery and "was at a very low point" when Sister Margaret Mary invited her to come to Mother's room to read a letter she had received from an abbess at another Poor Clare monastery in India.

Mother was propped up on pillows, reclining in her bed when Antoinette cautiously entered the cell. With little ceremony, the sister read the letter aloud. Addressed to Mother Angelica, the note urgently requested that Our Lady of the Angels Monastery provide nuns to populate the very first monastery of the order in Troyes, France, home to the chapel where the Poor Clares of Perpetual Adoration began worshipping their Lord in 1856. After years of being in the hands of laypeople, the monastery in Troyes was to be returned to the order. Mother Angelica had already sent one nun, Sister Faustina, to France, but more were now needed. Having read the letter and performed her duty, Sister Antoinette vacated the room.

In her absence, Margaret Mary told Mother how Sister Antoinette longed to go to France. Actually, in her role as community historian, Sister Antoinette just wanted to spend some quality time in the French monastery's archives. Within minutes the nun was called back to Mother's room via intercom.

"When I opened the door, Mother's face was like the sunshine—glowing," Sister Antoinette remembered.

Angelica extended a hand to the worried sister. Then with great effort she managed to say, "Go to France. You have my blessing and we will always be one in heart."

Antoinette abandoned the work on her desk, packed her bags, and on January 21, 2005, left for a three-month stay in France, just to try it out. The unexpected change of plans proved providential and probably spared Sister Antoinette much heartache in the days to come.

By March the sisters were informed, in a letter from the bishop of Nagasaki, that there was to be no new monastery in his diocese. The bishop's priest council had vetoed the idea, believing the sisters would have difficulty attracting vocations in Japan. "Maybe we don't have enough faith," he wrote.

For Sisters Margaret Mary and Gabriel, the loss of the Japanese foundation was a severe blow.

April saw the election of a new pope: Joseph Ratzinger, who took the name Benedict XVI. In his previous position, as head of the Congregation for the Doctrine of the Faith, Cardinal Ratzinger had been a great admirer of Mother Angelica and a defender of her work. When he assumed the Chair of Peter, the nuns and Mother jubilated. But tears would fill their eyes only a month later when a crop of their sisters departed for Phoenix, Arizona.

Mother Angelica, in her habit, was rolled out onto the monastery carport to bid farewell to her westbound daughters on May 1, 2005. For most of the forty nuns, the parting was sorrowful. Sisters Marie Andre, Mary Fidelis, Marie St. Paul, Mary Joanna, and Esther Marie— the self-described "Phoenix Phive"—lined up before Mother one last time. She blessed each of the nuns as they boarded the gold minivan that would take them to their new desert home. For the Phoenix sisters, having endured so much to get to that point, the departure was a relief, if a bittersweet one. So many friends were left in the rearview mirror. As they pulled away, Sister Catherine, the vicar, propelled Mother Angelica's wheelchair alongside the van, following it to the very edge of the enclosure gate. Mother was practically giddy. More of her daughters were leaving—on their way to complete her mission to create new "Eucharistic thrones" in other places. The Lord was indeed scattering them "like rose petals across the land."

The departure of the Phoenix sisters was one of the rare occasions when Mother abandoned her room. The next major occasion was the release of my biography, *Mother Angelica: The Remarkable Story of a Nun, Her Nerve, and a Network of Miracles*, in September. There was talk of Mother joining me in New York for a kickoff event, but her health precluded such a journey. Instead, we held the first event for the biography in the monastery gift shop and pilgrimage center, the Castel San Miguel. Even on the grounds of her monastery, Mother's appearance could not be confirmed until the very last minute. Her mobility continued to decrease. But somehow she managed to make it over to the Castel, wave to well-wishers, and spend hours in the parlor of her monastery greeting visitors who had come up for the big day. Many people burst into tears at the mere sight of her. It was to be the last real public event Mother would attend. From that point onward, her bedroom truly became her entire world.

The flight of so many sisters to other foundations was keenly felt within the walls of Our Lady of the Angels. It somehow threw off the balance of the house. In short order two camps began to emerge—a subtle and not-so-subtle split in the monastery.

The older professed sisters, many of whom had joined the community decades earlier, cleaved to Mother and could often be found nesting in her room. Some of the older sisters would candidly admit that they didn't care for the gargantuan size of the Hanceville monastery and pined for the intimate confines of the old Birmingham house. Some of them kept to themselves and had little interaction with their younger counterparts. Then there were the younger nuns, whose ranks seemed to be swelling all the time. Sister Catherine, in her role as vicar of the monastery, generously welcomed new applicants to the community. So many were admitted that four rooms had to be added to the cloister in 2005 to accommodate the overflow. As sweet as these young sisters were, they were strangers to the professed nuns, youngsters who lacked the history and habits that came with being at Our Lady of the Angels for decades.

Mother Angelica was conscious of the split in the house and even raised it with me in unguarded moments on a few occasions. One of her nuns accurately captured the dynamic: "Mother tried to give the solemn professed a little more attention because they were no longer an intimate, family group [as they had been in the tightly packed monastery in Birmingham]. There were thirty more nuns around . . . There was a lot of competition among the older and younger sisters at that time. The older nuns felt they were being left behind and Mother was being torn from them. The younger nuns wanted time with her. They did the same things siblings do: they competed for attention. Mother tried to do the best she could, but she was pulled in so many directions between building the Shrine, EWTN, and the forty sisters."

Since founding Our Lady of the Angels in 1962, Mother Angelica used her daily lessons to the professed nuns to impart the "family spirit" she envisioned for the community, advising them that "all members of a family must feel they have a right to express their opinion without bringing condemnation down on themselves. We must make allowance for differences in character traits and tastes and never feel because a sister thinks differently than we do that she doesn't love us. We must be mature women. Every one of us has idiosyncrasies that we must be big enough to forbear and overlook. . . . We must be able to accept our sisters where they are and love them."

When sisters failed to live up to this ideal, Mother took it personally and felt it deeply.

"I remember Mother crying in Birmingham at the table one day at lesson. You could hear a pin drop," recalled a sister who asked not to be identified. "Some sisters had criticized her and I remember Reverend Mother saying, 'What have I done to make you so ungrateful . . . to complain and criticize and be so disobedient?' She was so sad. She was concerned about our souls. 'You're religious and you're called to great things,' she said. 'Being disobedient and critical is not among them.'"

Petty personal failings gave way to larger, more complex problems, particularly in the confines of a religious community, where everything was magnified. Mother repeatedly warned the sisters about the "lack of charity" and the "childishness" she saw in the halls of the cloister. One of the younger sisters remembered Mother saying,

"It won't be the bishops or a cardinal who will destroy this community; it will be you. Tend to your souls, your spiritual lives."

The failure to heed Mother's warnings would in time explode into a full domestic conflict with disastrous results.

Strong-Willed Sisters

"THE LORD HAS BLESSED ME with strong-willed sisters—but thank God, my will is stronger," Mother Angelica once told me. Her sisters were buoyant, plucky, and, for contemplatives, amazingly outspoken. Like their abbess they conformed to the ideal of the contemplative life but managed to preserve their individual spark. It was Mother's larger-than-life presence and her tenacity that kept the diverse cloister in order and forged a unity among the nuns. Though Mother was still officially abbess of the monastery and could not be more revered, the situation in the house had obviously changed. As she physically retreated from the nuns' daily life, no longer appearing at community meals or prayer times due to her infirmity, the sisters turned elsewhere for leadership.

Sister Catherine was the elected vicar of Our Lady of the Angels and, while Mother was in her impaired state, the de facto superior of the house. A dedicated worker, she radiated a laid-back abandon—a willingness to go where God called her. A native of Louisiana's Cajun country, Catherine was open to the nudges of the Holy Spirit. She was partial to mystics, and had a talent for spontaneously making decisions big and small. As vicar she sought to form joyful sisters and maintain a peaceful, happy house where vocations could thrive. A good deal of her time was spent forming the young sisters as she had trained the middle generation of nuns in the community (some of whom had departed to lead other foundations). She was the type of nun who cared nothing for appearances. If Sister Catherine was working on a project and accidentally spilled something on the front of her habit, she'd acknowledge the stain, laugh it off, and sprint into the parlor to meet a visiting Church dignitary. She was relaxed, accessible, and very human. A great majority of the young sisters looked up to Catherine, as did many of the older nuns. But among a few of the senior professed sisters there were questions about Catherine's leadership.

In some quarters of the monastery, some of the older nuns began voicing concerns about the direction of things. They felt increasingly marginalized as the numbers of the younger religious grew, and they were vexed by some of the devotions proliferating inside the house.

In Mother's room was the nun whom the older sisters thought might deliver them from all of this and provide a leadership alternative to Sister Catherine.

Sister Margaret Mary seemed to live at Mother Angelica's side from the time she entered Our Lady of

the Angels. With a devoted fussiness, she kept a watchful eye on Mother's health and just about everything else.
For years, she often traveled with Mother and could be
seen trailing after her with a Thermos of tea and any required medications. A former Poor Clare Colletine, the
Michigan native often wore a wearied expression—as if
she were suddenly afflicted by a pain she was too polite
to share.

With intimates, Sister Margaret Mary was capable
of unleashing an explosive laugh and told stories with
great relish. But she could also be exacting and particular. Whether it was the design of the marble floor in
the chapel or the drape of Mother's veil, Margaret Mary
liked things just so. Demonstrating both her good taste
and her influence on Mother, the nun was responsible
for many of the architectural flourishes and furnishings throughout the Hanceville monastery and chapel.
Mother Angelica loved Margaret Mary, appreciated her
refined sensibility, and often indulged it. It was Sister
Margaret Mary who encouraged the community's return
to the traditional habit in the early 1990s, and she was
also a determined supporter of Mother's efforts to return
the community liturgy to its Latin roots. She was a nun
who enjoyed formality, order, and compliance with the
rules. Owing to her care of Mother, Margaret Mary was
not an active part of the wider community life and spent
much of her day in Mother's cell, or in her own, according to sisters who were interviewed.

Quiet grudges and hard feelings festered over fairly minuscule issues throughout the monastery. Though in the context of a confined cloister, the minuscule quickly becomes colossal.

Due to Mother's condition and her limited knowledge of the cloister at large, all the sisters were instructed to go to the vicar, Sister Catherine, to secure any "permissions" they might need. Permissions were required for everything from buying personal items to speaking to friends in the parlor, to securing exemptions from community prayer or meals.

Several of the younger sisters, in interviews, contended that a handful of the older nuns were "going directly to Mother Angelica for permissions. Mother always allowed them to do whatever they asked. . . . She was partial to the sisters she knew and was more comfortable with." Another sister charged that the nuns closest to Mother were "ignoring Sister Catherine's authority."

For their part, the older nuns felt that Sister Catherine showed a preference for the younger community members. This seems only reasonable since Catherine had trained them from the time they had entered the monastery and had more daily access to the younger sisters than to those surrounding Mother. Nevertheless, the perception among the senior professed was that Sister Catherine had "left the older sisters out in the cold." The way she had allowed the Arizona foundation to seek the blessing of the older nuns "as an afterthought" also left a bitter taste in certain seasoned mouths.

Sister Catherine "did whatever she felt like doing, totally disregarding the chapter [of elder nuns]," one sister complained. In interviews, Sister Catherine vigorously denied this assertion and pointed out that she not only required the Arizona nuns to go to the chapter for permission, but that she had convened the meeting herself. The main gripe against Sister Catherine—the principal thorn in the professed nuns' sides—was the vicar's affection for, and propagation of, a devotion known as "the Divine Will."

Adherents of this devotion, rooted in the writings of the Servant of God, Luisa Piccarreta, practice "living in the Divine Will" of God. In the late nineteenth century, Piccarreta suffered extreme pains and body rigidity that could be relieved only by the blessing of a priest. The Italian mystic claimed to have seen Jesus repeatedly, starting in her teen years, and to have received messages from Him for decades. In 1898, a confessor compelled Piccarreta to preserve in writing all her dialogues with the Savior. She would continue writing until 1938, producing thirty-six volumes collectively called *The Book of Heaven*. As of this writing, Piccarreta's cause for sainthood is under consideration by the Vatican, and her writings are still being scrutinized by the Holy See for theological errors.

Sister Catherine was first exposed to "the Divine

Will" when a sister and her grandmother shared the Piccarreta books with her. According to Catherine, "Mother spoke to me about the Divine Will three or four times before the stroke, and she was okay with us reading it."

The vicar gave copies of Piccarreta's books to the younger sisters who were interested, and would occasionally teach the devotion during lessons. According to a number of the younger sisters, Catherine taught that the Divine Will was a devotion like any other, which sisters were free to read or not. But no matter what they decided, they "were not to discuss it or impose it on anyone," one sister confided.

In the reckoning of the older nuns, the Divine Will was "propaganda spread among the young sisters." To them, Sister Catherine had imported a foreign spirituality into their cloister, a devotion being observed by a growing number of young sisters. This perception furthered the estrangement between the elder and younger members of the monastery. It would take a number of years for these suppressed resentments to rise to the surface, but they were palpable nonetheless.

By 2006, Mother Angelica had settled into the situation God had allowed her. She would pray with the sisters, occasionally watch TV, and attempt to preserve a sense of tranquility and quiet in her room. One nun recalled, at the time, watching a series entitled *Heaven* that Mother had recorded in the mid-1980s. The abbess was laughing at herself on TV, genuinely amused by the show, when another sister walked in attempting to engage her in conversation. Mother's words were few and far between at that point, and she found the lunch overture distracting.

"I came in to talk to you," the sister said trying to draw Mother out, "but you don't have to talk if you don't want to."

"I won't," Mother said, looking up from the TV, and she promptly began laughing. All Mother really wanted was quiet. But there was to be none for her. Something was rotten in Our Lady of the Angels Monastery—the roof.

In what could be viewed as a metaphor for the acrimony unfolding within its walls, the monastery roof started leaking in 2006. Water stains began appearing on the laundry ceiling, and by early 2007 water was streaming down the marble columns in the chapel. Apparently, the construction company had used plywood covered with plastic to assemble the roof. The material did not permit moisture to escape, literally rotting the ceilings of the building.

As the nuns frantically sought to repair their leaky roof, a new bishop arrived in Birmingham, in October of 2007. Bishop Robert Baker, formerly of Charleston, South Carolina, was a gentle, sober soul who had great affection for Mother Angelica and her sisters. The day after the bishop's installation, the pope's representative in the United States, Archbishop Pietro Sambi, and the newly minted bishop visited the nuns for lunch at the monastery. Mother Angelica, through great effort, wore her full habit and was situated in a wheelchair to greet the esteemed visitors.

Archbishop Sambi was quite taken with Mother and held her hand repeatedly throughout their time together. After lunch and a tour of the monastery, Sambi announced, "I have spent my day at the network [EWTN] and here and I have come away enriched by the spirit of Mother Angelica. You all are called to expand that spirit everywhere." It was a charge many of the sisters took to heart, though at that moment there was a debate rising within the monastery about what constituted "Mother's spirit," and who best embodied it going forward.

Sister Catherine and Sister Margaret Mary in general terms became the representatives of the two visions of Mother's spirit within the monastery. It was not a major scandal or even nefarious doings that divided Our Lady of the Angels, but a fairly common phenomenon whenever a founder or foundress recedes from a religious community. Having known these sisters for the better part of nineteen years and seen their great gifts and human quirks up close, I believe that what dogged Our Lady of the Angels was a tug-of-war over the future direction of the foundation, and perhaps a touch of ambition, but nothing more.

When a founder leaves a community there is always a reevaluation of the core charism and vision, a time when the members regroup to examine what is worth preserving, what is essential, in the aftermath of the prime mover. The consensus of many of the sisters I interviewed was that these two strong-willed women personified dual aspects of Mother Angelica's charism and spirit. On the one hand, Sister Catherine reflected Mother's freewheeling, Spirit-driven leadership; she was not averse to sudden moves when God took things in a new direction. In total accord with Mother Angelica's vision for community life, she craved a "family monastery" that was warm and joyous. And save for a handful of sisters, on the whole, the occupants of Our Lady of the Angels were a happy and busy group.

Sister Margaret Mary represented the latter-day Mother Angelica, after she had recalibrated her monastic approach, restoring many of the traditional practices and protocols of religious life that she had forsaken in her earlier days. Margaret Mary emphasized decorum and obedience and was annoyed by the whimsical nature of some of Sister Catherine's decisions.

The contrasting personalities of these two nuns and their disparate approaches to monastic life could only find harmony in Mother Angelica. If they could have come together and found some happy medium, the situation might have been salvageable. More than anything else, it was a clash of styles and approaches that divided them. On the things that mattered, like the Latin liturgy or devotion to the Eucharist, Sisters Catherine and Margaret Mary probably agreed more than they disagreed.

But both sisters had learned leadership from Mother Angelica; at Our Lady of the Angels Monastery there could be only one superior, and her word would be final. Mother had imparted this teaching to the sisters for decades during their private daily lessons. In retrospect those teachings have a prophetic air—like this one she showed me from the 1980s:

"Whatever my superior says I should be doing at that moment is the most Holy Will of God. Not up for discussion. When you realize that, sisters, you have made a giant step. If you begin to question why Reverend Mother does this or that then you've gone a long way down. . . . I wonder sometimes if you didn't have a strong superior in front of you whether you would just turn into a little, bickering bunch of women."

Sister Catherine as vicar recognized that some of the older sisters, including Sister Margaret Mary, had grown attached to Mother Angelica. Rather than invite challenges to her leadership or cause greater tension in the house, Sister Catherine allowed Margaret Mary and some of the other sisters to continue living as they had for many years, in Mother's orbit and in her room. This nonconfrontational, "live and let live" approach was the vicar's way. She preferred the gentle touch to the sledge-hammer. As Catherine went about attending to the affairs of the monastery and the welfare of the sisters at large, a small group of the professed nuns collectively second-guessed her actions.

In a notebook one of the sisters shared with me from the early days of the monastery, Mother Angelica warned her protégés during a lesson: "Sisters, whenever you find yourself busy about what Sister So-and-So is doing or where she is—then you are in serious trouble with critical thoughts, jealousies, anger, and ambition. That's when you have hell on earth, in yourself and all around you. When a community comes to that, they have hell on earth."

A resistance movement of sorts, to counter the per-ceived wrongs in the monastery, convened regularly in Mother's room. There, a select group of the older sisters congregated to share news and plan for the future. Per-haps it was their attempt to re-create the cozy intimacy they once enjoyed before the new monastery was built—before unfamiliar young faces had distanced them from one another and from the Mother they so cherished.

Over Angelica's bed they spoke of the errors being committed throughout the house and the dissemina-tion of the Divine Will devotion that they considered "heresy." They also raised questions about the decisions made by Sister Catherine. Mother Angelica, who always hated cloister gossip, did her best to put it down—even in her weakened state.

One nun who regularly spent the night in Mother's room shared a telling anecdote. One morning in the ab-bess's cell, she and another nun were going about their duties when they began bad-mouthing a sister who was not present. "I noticed that as soon as I mentioned the faults of this other sister, Mother's face hardened. I should have kept quiet," the sister said. "As I was begging her to take her medications she said, 'Support! Support!' . . . it was the correction I needed, as my behavior was definitely not that of a supportive sister."

Confined to her bed, Mother had to listen to similar chatter day and night. But even in her impaired state, Angelica attempted to discipline and warn her charges. At that same time, in July of 2008, Sister Grace Marie, an Anglican convert who had been with the order for twenty-five years, left Hanceville to start yet another new foundation—this one in San Antonio, Texas.

A year earlier, during a Mass of solemn profession at the monastery, Grace Marie had been touched by the beauty of the Anglican Use liturgy she had known as a girl. The priest who had come to celebrate the Mass invited the nuns to start a new foundation in San Antonio. All at once a group of sisters came together, believing that God was calling them to establish a new monastery. Grace Marie, having spent so much time near Mother, could not envision going away, but she took the inspiration to Angelica nonetheless.

"Sister Margaret Mary left the room," Grace Marie recalled. "I knelt down next to Mother and said, 'I need to ask you something. This is new to me, and it just came up and the Lord has put it on my heart. I feel like the Lord is asking me to start a new foundation.'

I was in tears because the thought of leaving her was troubling. Suddenly, it was like the old Mother was back. She looked at me and put her hand on my arm and squeezed it, saying, 'I understand and I bless you.' I honestly thought she'd say no. I went into shock."

Shock or no, Sister Grace Marie took her inspiration to the chapter of professed nuns and without fuss or opposition swiftly received their support for the San Antonio foundation. From there, things really sailed along. Only six weeks after asking the Vatican for permission to proceed with plans for the new monastery, the sisters received the go-ahead.

Mother blessed each of the five San Antonio–bound nuns at her bedside. With the departure of Sisters Grace Marie, Marie St. Clare, Rose Marie, Elizabeth Marie, and Mary Peter, the Hanceville monastery was deprived of nuns who "bridged the gap" between the two opposing sides within the house. The easy time they had procuring the blessing of the professed nuns for their foundation (as opposed to the conflict the Arizona sisters aroused) indicates the esteem the older nuns had for this crop of sisters. A few of the San Antonio nuns suggested to me that they saw themselves as "buffers" between their conflicted sisters. With the buffers gone, anxieties increased, and talk of a coming election in the monastery the following May dominated conversation.

In Mother's room emotions ran high and there were periods of "great tension." Mother Angelica could be sul-

len and often fell silent during this period. She was preoccupied by all she heard and saw.

On one occasion, four of the sisters were in her room
watching an *I Love Lucy* episode. As they laughed and
went about their work, a sister who was present told me,
"Mother was extremely serious and quiet, not watching
TV at all. She held her blanket real tight, close to her
neck, and in a loud, clear voice told the sisters, 'I'm trying to protect you!' The sisters left her alone. She closed
her eyes—but she was not sleeping." Angelica was very
likely praying, using the last power within her reach to
encourage peace in the fractious monastery—or at least
the monastery in her sight line.

Mother Angelica was well aware of the challenges,
and the personalities at play. One of the nuns told me
that in 1997, at lesson, Angelica glared at them, saying:
"I'm amazed at sisters' wills. I do give in to you too much,
because I know if I don't you're either going to pout or
get angry—that's a fault of mine. But I have halfway
determined that it has to end. I've got to say no to you
because you could end up in purgatory or somewhere
else when you always do what you want to do."

"She used to get so irritated during lessons," Sister
St. John remembered. "She'd say, 'Sisters, the jealousies,
the backbiting is so stupid—if you only knew the Love
of God, His individual love for you, you wouldn't waste
your time doing this.'"

With the monastery deprived of Mother's voice, a

quiet struggle went on inside Our Lady of the Angels for the better part of a year leading up to the May election for vicar and chapter members. It was a veiled campaign, conducted in murmurs and via clandestine meetings. One band of sisters stood with the current vicar, Sister Catherine, while another group rallied around Sister Margaret Mary in Mother's cell.

The arm-twisting and the search for votes grew intense. Certain sisters who were undecided or still supporting Sister Catherine were stopped in hallways or in the refectory and convinced to back Margaret Mary. The main argument used against Sister Catherine was her dissemination of the Divine Will devotion, and the ubiquity of the books throughout the cloister. The Divine Will became the rallying point for the opponents of the vicar, and convincing evidence that she was leading the nuns down a spiritual path Mother never intended.

The truth is that most of the sisters had private devotions, including Sister Margaret Mary. It was she who convinced Mother to record the Chaplet of St. Michael the Archangel on television in 2006, even though those invocations had never been part of Mother's prayer life. Ironically, the chaplet was based on the private revelations of a Carmelite visionary. And despite the charges that the Divine Will was heretical, the bishop of Birmingham, Robert Baker, had, according to Sister Catherine, granted her permission to read the books and had read some of them himself.

In a letter to EWTN on October 4, 2003, the Congregation for the Doctrine of the Faith confirmed that the writings of Luisa Piccarreta were still being studied due to the advancement of her cause for canonization. The CDF said that the works enjoyed "neither the approbation, nor the condemnation" of the Vatican and that there would be "no pronouncement on the writings" at that time. Still, in the hothouse of the monastery's election season, the Divine Will was a convenient and useful political football.

Sister Catherine recalls going into Mother's room a week before the elections to wish her good night, as was her routine. The vicar would sing a little song to Mother, who'd finish the lyrics or sometimes sing along. This one particular night, Catherine believes she interrupted a conversation the other nuns were having in the room about the elections and her leadership. Mother Angelica's actions were out of character. "Mother was more sympathetic with me than usual," Catherine told me. "She stroked my head and held my hand, smiling sweetly. And while she was doing it, she shot some of the others there a nasty look. The way she was acting was not normal. She was clearly not pleased with what was happening in there."

All parties knew it was going to be a close election, and with so many professed sisters in other places starting new foundations, every vote counted. Even Mother's first spiritual daughter, Sister Joseph, was subjected to heavy lobbying. The eighty-six-year-old had been suffering from nerve damage and had blood sugar problems for many years. She was flustered by what she saw in the monastery. Initially, Joseph intended to vote for Sister Catherine, as she had in the last three elections. But in the days leading up to the balloting, another sister convinced her to switch allegiances. Would that be enough support to cinch the election for Sister Margaret Mary? The nuns in Mother's room counted the votes they believed they had and prayed for success.

Mother Angelica simply closed her eyes. Whether she was tired or decided it was time to shut out the din of the unwelcome election talk, she retreated to the only place she could find peace: in slumber.

A New Vicar

BISHOP BAKER ARRIVED in the largest parlor of the monastery to observe the community elections in early May 2009. All the professed sisters living under the roof assembled in the parlor. The heightened anticipation created an oppressive atmosphere. Sister Catherine asked one of the extern nuns to phone Mother Angelica's room to see if she was ready to vote. Following orders, the nun went into the hall and rang Mother's extension.

"She's all ready," the extern announced, returning to the parlor.

"Who are you going to choose to collect Mother's vote?" the bishop asked.

"*Sister!*" a nun's voice hissed frantically from somewhere in the parlor.

As if prompted, Sister Margaret Mary rose. "Mother Angelica had decided not to vote," she said calmly.

This came as a shock to the bishop, the vicar, and some of the other nuns, but they decided to proceed with the election anyway. The sisters filled out their ballots, dropped them into the collection box, and awaited the result. The two nuns appointed to count the votes executed their duty.

Following the vote count, Sister Catherine and Sister Margaret Mary processed to Mother Angelica's room to share the outcome. Sister Margaret Mary had been elected vicar by one vote. A nun in the room reported, "When Mother heard the news she put her head down and shook it back and forth. And it went downhill from there."

The new vicar wasted no time calling chapter meetings to reconsider the vocations of some of the younger nuns in the monastery—particularly those who practiced the Divine Will. Some would be asked to leave the community. Two nuns departed shortly after elections. Five were gone by July.

A professed sister who opposed Margaret Mary's election said of her leadership, "She really felt that she was doing the right thing and saving the community—and the older sisters were backing her up. Half the community was with Catherine and half was with Margaret Mary. That sounds terrible, but that's what happened. Some sisters were fearful of her."

Sister Margaret Mary could be prone to drama,

complete with tears and a frequently raised voice. Sisters recall the vicar chastising Sister Catherine in front of the community for perceived errors her predecessor had committed. Other sisters remember her addressing the nuns in a "high singsong voice as if we were kindergarten children in need of instruction . . . We were grown women. It was insulting."

In matters large and small, esthetics and uniformity in the monastery became major concerns for the new vicar. Since moving into the house in 1999, sisters had rearranged the furnishings in their private quarters as they saw fit. Once she became vicar, Sister Margaret Mary directed all the nuns to restore their cells, and the furniture therein, to the original configuration, "as Mother Angelica had designed them." Most of the sisters knew it was Sister Margaret Mary who had designed the cells with Mother's approval.

Purging the monastery of the Divine Will books became a chief priority even though, according to several nuns interviewed, only five or six nuns were actively reading it. Margaret Mary fumed about the devotion at length, insisting that the Divine Will "was not Eucharistic" and was "a heresy." One of the extern nuns remembers the vicar instructing her to stop selling the writings of Luisa Piccarreta in the nuns' gift shop and told her that the book should not even be on the monastery grounds. The new rules and the vanishing postulants created an atmosphere of anxiety and worry.

"This black cloud filled the whole place," one former sister said of that postelection monastery. "Depression was everywhere. I remember talking to a junior professed in the bursar's office and she said, 'When is this going to end? I feel so heavy and oppressed.'"

Sisters would retreat to the extern quarters just to escape the emotional pressure of the monastery.

After one of the hastily called chapter meetings, Sister Joseph walked into the sewing room, fright written all over her face, according to a sister who worked with her. The old nun's eyes were wide and her hands trembled. "I can't take this anymore," she told the younger nun.

Mother's health took a turn for the worse after the elections. "During that time she got very sick," a caretaker in her room told me. "Sometimes it would take two hours to administer her medicine. She would hold the medicine in her mouth and she wouldn't swallow. Mother slept all the time, and she refused to eat and drink . . . it was almost like an intentional starvation."

The nuns were so concerned about the rapid decline of Mother's health that a casket was prepared—complete with Angelica's coat of arms—and stowed in the abbess's office. But Mother had no need of the things. Her mission continued.

Right after elections, a couple of nuns proposed starting yet another new foundation, out west. Once word reached Sister Margaret Mary's ear, she called the entire community together and announced definitively that there would be no new foundations, "so forget about it." Scalded by the reaction and all they had witnessed, a group of nuns resolved to send a letter to Rome, questioning the validity of the vicar's election.

Their contention was that canon law required *all* the professed sisters of Our Lady of the Angels Monastery to vote in the election, including those who had gone to start new monasteries not yet established. Since the nuns in San Antonio, Phoenix, and France were not called to the motherhouse for the election, they reasoned, the election must be invalid. And then there was the question of Mother Angelica's abstention from the vote. On these grounds, a group of the nuns hoped the Vatican would invalidate Margaret Mary's election and require the sisters to vote again en masse. Only weeks after the election, the nuns mailed their letter of complaint to Rome. The response was less than predictable.

Rome affirmed the election of Sister Margaret Mary, and on July 13, 2009, Bishop Robert Baker appeared at the monastery with a startling announcement. After receiving several letters from members of Our Lady of the Angels Monastery, the Holy See had authorized a visitation: a formal investigation of the community that would commence in August of that year. The bishop also informed the community that the Vatican congregation responsible for religious had decreed that chapter meetings and the expulsion of sisters were to cease immediately.

On July 19, 2009, the nuns received an early warning
of what was to come. Sister Joseph, looking drawn and
frail, carefully teetered into one of the bathrooms off the
monastery hallway during lunch. She would not exit of
her own volition. Joseph was discovered later, slouched
against the bathroom wall. Her death was instantaneous, likely the result of a blood clot. Sisters lining the
hallway broke into tears when they saw the old nun's
body slumped on the tile. "Lord, why did she have to
die now?" one sister exclaimed in a moment of candor.
"We needed that vote." But Sister Mary Joseph, Mother
Angelica's first spiritual daughter in Canton, Ohio, and
a founding member of Our Lady of the Angels, would
vote no more.

Mother Angelica grieved the passing of her friend.
She was very distant at that time, lost in her thoughts
and withdrawn. "Pain is part of our sanctification,"
Mother once told me. "How are we going to be like the
Lord if we don't have the opportunity to shed those
things that are controlling us, diverting us from holiness. Pain is that opportunity." Such opportunities surrounded Mother Angelica in the summer of 2009 and
she knew it.

One afternoon, Sister Veronica, a young nun assisting
Mother in her room, asked the abbess to do something
physically difficult for her—a real sacrifice. Angelica
turned her eyes up to the crucifix on the wall. "I could
see her praying and she put her arms out like Jesus on

the cross," Sister Veronica remembered, "and she just gave me a smile that sort of said, 'I have to live with this.' Just watching her total union with the Lord was awesome."

Eight years earlier she had asked God to allow her "to stay until the worst is over." Now pinioned to her bed, arms outstretched, she physically mimicked the One who had stayed beyond "the worst"—offering all she had to Him and to her community.

CHAPTER 3

The Mystic of Hanceville

You cannot arrive at transforming union without spiritual and mental suffering because transformation demands it. You're not able to face God in your present state—so you've got to go through physical suffering or spiritual suffering. Dryness, desolation, the darkness of faith; all of this is painful.

—MOTHER ANGELICA

SHE ALWAYS HAD a supernatural air about her. Whether on television when she would inhale deeply and suddenly speak in that deliberate, inspired cadence, or when she glanced over her shoulder and caught the Child Jesus running down the monastery halls, Mother Angelica had experiences—saw and heard things—most did not.

Her awareness of the eternal, the connection between this life and the life to come, was highly refined. As the end of her life approached, Mother's receptiveness to God's will and the need to comply with it in "the present moment" only intensified.

Sister Mary Peter tells the story of going into Mother's room and asking the abbess if she wanted to get into her wheelchair and venture out onto the patio for some fresh air. Mother instantly responded, "No, this is where I am supposed to be. In this room." The statement conveyed a resigned sense that she understood the bedroom to be part of her spiritual lot—the final arena where she would prove her sanctity, the place where God desired that she work out her salvation. The isolated cell at the far edge of Our Lady of the Angels Monastery was God's will for her. That room would be the backdrop for a number of supernatural occurrences and manifestations—some of which Mother had encountered before.

From the time she was a young girl, Rita Rizzo had contact with the divine. "I think she is one of those chosen souls that has a clear vision of the supernatural," a sister who spent years caring for Mother in her room insisted.

It began with an incident on the streets of Canton, Ohio. Mother Angelica recalled crossing a busy street downtown to catch a bus. As she reached the center of the boulevard, a vehicle bore down on her. It was so close, she didn't know whether to run forward or back. With no time to clear the vehicle's path, she froze in fear and closed her eyes. "All of a sudden, it felt as if two hands under my arms picked me up—I can almost feel them when I talk about it," Mother told me. "And [they] put me on the island where the cars were parked."

Eyewitnesses said it was "a miracle," and that they had never seen "somebody jump so high before." Rita Rizzo considered the experience a brush with grace, a near disaster averted by a divine hand. It would be the first of many, many such encounters.

Through Rhoda Wise, the stout stigmatic and mystic Rita met in her youth, the girl had firsthand contact with someone considered to be in direct communication with God. Wise not only claimed to converse with Jesus and the saints, she also swore she saw them. Her physical manifestations—the spontaneously bleeding palms and blood-drenched forehead on Fridays—only lent credibility to Wise's claims. For the young Rita Rizzo Rhoda's experiences provided proof of God's existence and insight into His mysterious ways. From that time on Rita would never question supernatural phenomena. Seeing angels and saints or receiving direct messages from God were simply part of living a faithful life. These were things to be expected and accepted. Following her experience with Wise, and to her last days, Rita was receptive to promptings and visions others might dismiss or talk away.

Rhoda Wise also acquainted the young woman with the puzzling power of suffering. Wise considered herself "a victim soul," one who offers up personal sufferings and pain to God for the good of others. And though Mother Angelica never considered herself a victim soul, she would, in time, bear the marks of one. Her pain made her available to God and reliant upon Him. "Availability is letting God have His way, even when it brings us to the cross," Father Richard John Neuhaus, the revered intellectual, wrote. "For those who are available, life is at God's disposal, kept in readiness for what He may be up to."

After she entered religious life, the first signs of Sister Angelica's unique relationship with God began to emerge. She would envision the detailed plans for the Birmingham monastery on the wall of her cell in Ohio. Physical ailments and their disappearance would guide her journey from monastery to monastery. Then there is the fascinating story she shared with me late one night, near the end of a short interview session. It is from her days at the Canton monastery in the late 1950s, and has never appeared in print. It concerns Mother Angelica's uncle Nick Gianfrancesco, whom she appointed contractor for a grotto she was building in the monastery yard at the time. While Uncle Nick was off site, Sister Angelica authorized a bricklayer nicknamed Number Nine to place a "perfect" keystone at the top of the grotto.

That night at the work site, Uncle Nick discovered the keystone, which he had never seen before, grouted into place. He was not pleased.

"Where'd you get that?" Uncle Nick asked Angelica, exasperated, as he pointed to the triangular stone at the top of the arch.

"Isn't it wonderful? Number Nine put it there," answered Angelica.

"I already had one picked out."

"You weren't around, and I didn't know it was that important. I can't take it out now."

Uncle Nick's face turned the color of Chianti. "Okay, you don't want me to finish it! Fine!"

"For goodness' sake, Uncle Nick, I didn't say I didn't want you to finish it."

"Well, you can finish it yourself!" Uncle Nick deserted the job, stomping out of the cloister yard. Work continued without him.

Days later, an irritated Nick called the monastery.

"You didn't have to scare the hell out of me," he told Sister Angelica.

"What?" the confused nun asked.

"I don't appreciate the way you did it either."

"Uncle Nick, are you going bongo or something?" Angelica countered.

"No, you appeared to me last night at the edge of my bed and shook your finger at me," Uncle Nick continued. "You could have just said, 'Are you sorry?' and I would have said, 'Yes.' You didn't have to *appear* to me."

"Uncle Nick, I did not appear to you. I was sound asleep. Now I think you're being ridiculous."

"I'm coming back to finish the grotto!" Uncle Nick yelled through the receiver.

"Well, good for you," Angelica said, hanging up.

Aside from providing insight into Mother Angelica's colorful family, this is the first record of a supernatural occurrence involving the nun during her religious life. Verifying whether this was an authentic case of bilocation more than fifty years after the fact is impossible, and beyond the scope of this work. When I pressed Mother about whether she had any recollection of having "appeared" to her uncle, she said she did not.

Over the centuries saintly individuals from Padre Pio to Alphonsus Liguori to Anthony of Padua reputedly had the gift of bilocation: the ability to be in two places at the same time, and to appear even on foreign continents and in secure locations. Liguori, for instance, went into a trance before Mass and visited the dying Pope Clement XIV in faraway Rome. Padre Pio would drift into a deep sleep and upon awaking claim to have traveled to other countries, including America. Later his "visits" were confirmed by multiple people in those foreign lands.

Over the years, Our Lady of the Angels Monastery has received letters from people who assert that Mother Angelica has visited them in a moment of distress. A letter from a girl in South America suggested that she clearly saw Mother Angelica at the foot of her bed one night. A truck driver, who was at a low point in his life, wrote that Mother Angelica appeared in the cab of his rig, on the seat next to him, as he was driving one evening. When confronted with these letters, Mother laughed and could only hazard the guess that the visitations might have been her guardian angel taking on her mien.

Whether these appearances were products of active imaginations or supernatural events can only be determined through extensive study. My efforts to track down the authors of the two letters mentioned above proved fruitless. But for some of the sisters closest to Mother, no proof or further explanations are necessary.

"I feel in my heart that when she is sleeping deeply, she is bilocating," Sister Gabriel consistently maintained. "So I try not to wake her when she is in a deep sleep." Even at rest Angelica seemed to be battling, her head moving from side to side, her legs shifting suddenly. And though no one can definitively say whether Mother has traveled to other locations while lying in her bed, her prayers have yielded equally fantastic feats, allowing her to reach the hearts of people all over the world.

In a 2012 letter, Juanita Threlkeld wrote:

> As a small business owner and a mother of two boys of school age . . . I do think of Mother often and pray that she is resting comfortably. I know she is still bringing her light and love, Jesus, to the world. Recently, I have been having some issues with my life and faith in general. I had a dream the other night and it was Mother who came to me and hugged me. She told me, in her classic

Mother Angelica voice, "Ya know, God loves you."
I woke with a feeling of calmness and a renewed
sense of hope. Thank you again, Mother!!

Rachel Bush was a Protestant who had been watching EWTN for years with her husband. She attended
Mass each Sunday and was even taking RCIA (Rite of
Christian Initiation of Adults) courses, but she still had
a deep reservation about converting:

> I wanted—needed the Eucharist. I had just one
> roadblock left: Mary. I never despised her or
> anything, but I didn't understand why Catholics
> venerate her so much. I had a dream one night
> that I was in a little chapel in front of a statue of
> Mary, with the candles around. I knelt and looked
> up at her and said, "What's so great about you?"
> Just then, Mother Angelica walked in and said,
> "Honey, if she's good enough for Jesus, isn't she
> good enough for you?" I woke up and bawled my
> eyes out, because I knew that I had to be Catholic,
> and that I had a mother in Mary.
>
> This was a little over five years ago, and I came
> into the Church. . . . It was the best decision I
> ever made.

The consolation of seeing beloved spiritual figures or
hearing a message from them was a grace Mother An-

gelica experienced many times throughout her life. The monastery history mentions Angelica visiting Cascia, Italy, where she viewed the incorrupt body of St. Rita. As she stared into the glass casket holding the remains of the saint, Mother believed that St. Rita's eyes opened and looked directly at her.

Saint Michael the Archangel was a repeat visitor to Mother, both at home and abroad over many years. An appearance by Saint Michael on a Vandiver, Alabama, mountaintop in 1990 convinced Mother that she had found the perfect spot to build a shortwave radio facility. Today, EWTN's shortwave station still stands on that very location.

During construction of the monastery in Birmingham in the early 1960s, some of the older sisters recall Mother telling them she heard singing at the construction site one day. Balancing on her crutches, Mother ambled up the hillside, following the sweet music. "What are those sisters doing up there?" she thought as she approached. Once she reached the nearly built monastery she found it vacant. "Mother called it Our Lady of the Angels Monastery, and there they were," Sister Emmanuel recounted, laughing a little too loudly.

Then there was the storied interaction with the Child Jesus at a shrine in Bogotá in 1996. According to Mother the statue of the Divino Niño came to life and instructed her to build Him "a temple." Years later, once the grand monastery had been erected in Hanceville, Alabama,

Mother claimed she saw the Child Jesus running up and down the chapel steps announcing, "This is my temple. This is my temple." Occasionally, she would also spy the Child dashing through the cloister hallways and at times clasping her about the legs.

After the stroke and the confinement to her room, Sister Catherine asked Mother one evening if she was still seeing the Divine Child. "No," she said solemnly. Deprived of the scant consolations she had received earlier, Angelica, during her last years would confront a supernatural visitor of a different sort.

The Enemy

DURING AN OTHERWISE quiet evening in her cell in 2009, Mother startled and sat straight up. The quick movement surprised Sister Gabriel, who was working near Mother's bed. Motionless, Angelica stared at a fixed spot across the room.

"What are you seeing, Mother? Saint Joseph?" Gabriel asked. Angelica shook her head.

"Saint Michael?"

Again she shook her head.

"The devil?"

Mother slowly nodded.

Sister Gabriel reached for a vial of holy water and splashed it in the direction of Mother's glance. With that, the abbess relaxed and lay back down.

It is not uncommon for those who have led virtuous lives to be taunted by dark forces at the end of their days. Just before they enter their long-sought-after reward, some are tempted one last time to doubt their faith and perhaps God Himself. In 2001, people were shocked to learn that Blessed Mother Teresa was the target of demonic attacks and received an exorcism shortly before her death. Far from casting doubt on her holiness, Archbishop Henry D'Souza (who authorized the exorcism) told CNN that he believed it was a proof of Mother Teresa's holiness: "When the person is being attacked by the devil and there is some evidence of that, it's further indication that the person has a very special holiness and therefore [is] a very special object of attack by Satan."

Mother Angelica may have been subjected to similar attacks in her last years.

On the evening of November 14, 2008, Sister Consolata was staying in Mother's room overnight. She was trying to fall asleep on a couch near Mother Angelica's bed when she was awoken around 9 p.m. by a temperature change in the room.

"It got freezing cold in there," Consolata said. "I could hardly breathe. It was as if there were one hundred pounds on top of me. I couldn't move, couldn't reach for my holy water or my rosary. I felt paralyzed except for my head. I started to pray." Mother was still awake, her head back on the pillow, running her fingers over the beads of her red rosary.

"The force of evil in the room was so strong, and it took all I had to pray and keep an eye on Mother." Sister Consolata wrote in her diary:

> Throughout all of this, Mother was awake and still, praying. . . . And then, out of the blue, a framed picture of Mother and Pope John Paul II on a column was thrown at an odd angle, into the center of the room. The other things on the column weren't moved. This can't be explained because there was a holy card standing up against the picture frame which didn't move at all—it was now leaning against a statue. The frame made a loud crash in the middle of the room—quite a distance away from the column where it previously stood. It was as if the frame was picked up and thrown directly at me. Had it not fallen in the middle of the floor, it would have hit me. Mother's head shot up but she didn't look around. My heart was pounding and I prayed extra hard for protection. The room was VERY tense. Around 10 PM, out of dead silence, while I was still "paralyzed" and getting quite nervous, Mother lifted her right hand and suddenly spoke. In a very loud, clear voice she said, "In the name of the Father, and of the Son, and of the Holy Spirit. Amen." She made the sign of the cross and kissed the crucifix on her rosary, put her head back down on the pillow, and promptly fell asleep. I could

suddenly move and the air was immediately normal again.

"Mother seemed to be aware of something else in the room but was not disturbed or bothered by it," Sister Consolata recalled. "She had *never* spoken that loudly and clearly in the middle of the night before. . . . I think she knew what was going on in the room and with me. She was praying."

These were not Mother's first encounters with "the Enemy," as she often called the devil. She once told me of waking to find an evil-looking "Carmelite nun" standing in her room. "She was not of God," Mother insisted. That particular dark vision did not return, but others would.

Sister Emmanuel related a story from the 1980s about Mother being woken one night in the Birmingham monastery. She had the feeling that someone was sitting on her bed. Propping herself up on an elbow to see the bottom of the bed, Mother believed she saw Satan perched on the edge of her mattress. "Oh it's you," Angelica said, then abruptly turned over and went back to sleep.

In the morning, Sister Regina entered with Mother's orange juice. Angelica told Regina of her uninvited visitor. "Where is he now?" Sister Regina asked.

"Right there. You just walked right through him," Mother answered, laughing hysterically.

But she wasn't laughing when "the Enemy" showed himself in 2009—in fact, she wasn't doing anything, and that was the problem. It was shortly after 4 a.m. in the morning, and Sister Augustine could not wake Mother Angelica. Her eyes were fluttering as if she were having a stroke or in some distress.

Panicked, Augustine roused Sister Margaret Mary. The two nuns tried to furiously shake Mother from her slumber. She showed no signs of waking. At that moment, lights flashed throughout the monastery. A buzzing sound echoed through the cloister halls. "The entire place turned an eerie green and there was a stench in the chapel—like sulfur," one sister remembered. "I had goose bumps up and down my arms."

Some sisters thought the flickering lights might be caused by a weather event, but when they checked outside, things were perfectly calm. After the light show, Mother opened her eyes and was her old self again.

"Those of us who experienced it felt the devil had Reverend Mother under some sort of control and when he released her, there was such a presence in that monastery," a sister told me. "It was an eerie feeling."

Whatever Mother Angelica grappled with in her sleep is not ours to know. It is like so many things of God: the vague outlines are ours to observe, but probe deeper and only mystery remains. While Mother struggled internally—perhaps spiritually battling an invisible opponent—the feuding in the monastery continued. The divisions that had gripped the house before the election remained in place.

In the lead-up to the Vatican investigation, Sister Margaret Mary and her supporters gathered in Mother's room each night to pray a special rosary to Our Lady of Success. They prayed that the coming Vatican visitation would produce a positive outcome. On their wish list: the removal of Sister Catherine and several sisters who they thought were distorting the life of the monastery.

To prepare for the visitation, a select corps of older sisters assembled in Mother's room. There they discussed what each sister would tell the visitators. The intention was to impress the Vatican investigators, who would not only meet with each nun at Our Lady of the Angels Monastery but also live among them for a week, observing the protocols and patterns of daily life. Sister Margaret Mary was anxious about the encounter and unsure of what to expect. She made certain that the house was glistening and busied herself tying up any loose ends.

Endless Love

IN THE FLEETING silence of her room, Mother Angelica rediscovered and renewed her love affair with Jesus in whatever ways she could.

"I was sitting on the sofa early one morning and Mother sat up in her bed with her eyes closed," Sister

Gabriel reminisced. "She nodded her head as if she was talking to somebody and her lips were moving. This went on for a minute or two and then she went back to sleep. I knew at that moment that she was talking to someone."

Sister Consolata offered similar memories. "You could see at times when you looked at her that she had just spoken to the Lord and He to her," Consolata said. "Anyone who spent time in that room could not question the supernatural activity of His presence in her life."

For all the wonders she witnessed and the many visions she was privy to, Mother Angelica's spiritual life was far from sunny. She told me in interviews that she often "experienced dryness in prayer," an absence of God's consolation—prayer without the contented feelings of having prayed. More often than not she lived by blind faith. Only after a painful episode or some wild, risky attempt to follow God's will would she experience a consoling vision, a message, or an angel on a mountaintop. But her daily devotion to the Beloved, while much less dramatic, was, for those who witnessed it, searingly memorable.

Mother Dolores Marie, who entered the Birmingham monastery in 1991, recalled seeing Angelica walk into the chapel after her live show in the late 1990s: "She would walk up the aisle and go lean on the altar. She'd place her arms on the altar and just look up at Jesus [in the Blessed Sacrament] and talk to Him interiorly."

Mother's diminished physical state did nothing to

decrease her intimacy with her Lord. In fact Angelica's love grew more intense.

Some mornings she would physically resist her care-takers as they tried to attend to her needs. But then the priest would enter the cell to deliver Communion to the abbess. She would instantly compose herself. "Ahhhh," she exhaled many times. Arms extended, defying the limitations of her speech, she more than once said, "You came to me," as if her One and Only had finally returned after a long separation. And He had.

"Her body would show how much love she had for Him," Sister Consolata confessed. "Those moments were more supernatural to me than some of the other odd things I witnessed."

On June 20, 2009, Mother had just completed her bath, and, consistent with her routine, she fell into a deep sleep. That day the entire community had recon-secrated itself to the Sacred Heart of Jesus, and to cap off the occasion the Blessed Sacrament—the Body and Blood of Jesus—was processed through every room of the monastery. So she wouldn't miss the visitation, the nun in Mother's room woke the abbess. She was peeved to have her sleep disturbed until she spotted the priest carrying the monstrance with the Sacred Host into her cell.

"When Mother saw the Blessed Sacrament, her face seemed to be aglow," a nun in the room recalled. "Her face was radiant and she was reaching, reaching for

Him. Finally, Jesus was lowered over her and she was able to touch the monstrance. She touched Him so lovingly, as though she was caressing Him, and then she gave Him a kiss. She never took her eyes off the Host, and watched closely as Father carried the monstrance out of the room. She remained facing the door without moving. The smile on her face was so special—a smile that expressed an intense longing and incredible peace. I've never experienced such an outburst of love as I did in that moment. She finally fell asleep, but each time she woke, she looked at me with tender affection. The whole atmosphere of the room was one of prayer and silence."

That was Mother's true objective in these trying years: to maintain a spirit of prayer and silence. But by August of 2009, her sisters were focused on the pending visitation that would determine their fate. Mother's room once again became the base of operations for the vicar, Sister Margaret Mary, and her councilors. On several occasions they assembled in Mother's room while the vicar read letters from Rome or from consulting canonists aloud. Mother had little patience for it all. She wanted to rest and pray—God would have to sort out the monastery. And though this cluster of sisters ardently begged God for Mother's recovery, clinging to the hope that she would miraculously rise from her bed and cure all that ailed the monastery, Mother only wanted quiet. At times when the conversations grew too clamorous or when she had simply had enough, the abbess would terminate the meetings herself with a forceful "Aw, shut up." Everyone got the message for the moment. But enduring peace and silence in Our Lady of the Angels Monastery would remain elusive.

CHAPTER 4

A Long, Loud Silence

The more silent we become interiorly, the closer we are getting to God. Did you ever hear a tree pushing out of the ground or the snow falling? Great things happen in silence.

—MOTHER ANGELICA, 1963

IT WAS PROBABLY not the way Mother Angelica wished to spend the sixty-fifth anniversary of her religious life. Nevertheless, on August 15, 2009, the feast day of the Assumption of the Virgin Mary, two strangers entered Our Lady of the Angels Monastery. They were the visitators sent by Rome to investigate the house: two nuns from different communities, superiors who had enormous respect for Mother Angelica and great concern about the welfare of the monastery and its reported troubles.

After two days, the visiting nuns had not been allowed to see Mother Angelica. When they conveyed their discomfort about being in the monastery without Mother's blessing, they were ushered into the abbess's room, accompanied by a cadre of sisters.

Mother sat up in bed as they entered, a joyous smile on her face. She eyed the two newcomers intensely, extending her hands toward them. Then in a voice strong and pure she said, "I am seeking the right ones. I was waiting for you to come." The ailing abbess clung to the hands of her guests. Sisters surrounding the bed burst into tears. So did the visitators. Mother's words at that time were rare, and on this day they could not have been more plain.

"It was a moment of clear understanding," said a sister who was in the room. "Mother knew what was going to happen to the community."

The abbess's warm welcome broke the ice and allowed the visitators to conduct their inquiry with the full cooperation of the nuns in house. Each sister had her moment to candidly relate her version of events to the visiting superiors, while community life and adoration of the Blessed Sacrament continued. Their adoration may have been the only constant amid all the upheaval, and a sure consolation to so many sisters who were unsettled by the process. One of Mother's lessons from the 1980s captures a sense of that moment: "As a contemplative order before the Blessed Sacrament, the Lord has really put a load on us, a real load—and that is to pray and sacrifice. Well, if He sends you the opportunities to sacrifice, you've got to take them. . . . You should not lose your union with God because union with God must be unceasing."

Mother maintained her union as best she could, looking forward, rarely back. When the sisters attempted to put EWTN on her television, Mother would object. She had little interest in watching what she had done, and aside from papal events and the occasional Mass, was not terribly interested in TV. Sister Gabriel told me that more often than not she wanted to watch Fox News. While viewing reports or opinion shows during her meals, she would occasionally blurt out "absolutely" or nod in affirmation after hearing a comment she found agreeable. The spunky fighter who had long added her voice to the debates of the day may have been silenced, but her concern and curiosity about the world beyond the cloister remained constant.

Sister Grace Marie remembers coming into the room to relieve Sister Margaret Mary one evening. Margaret Mary had flipped the television to EWTN and was making last-minute adjustments. "Okay Mother, I've got the network there and the volume is fine," Sister Margaret Mary cooed. Mother keenly watched Margaret Mary move about the room and finally exit. Once the door latched, she turned to Grace Marie. "Change the channel!" Mother said. The two nuns shared a belly laugh and watched the news.

The Vatican visitation to Our Lady of the Angels

Monastery would be the second Rome-sanctioned inquiry in less than a decade. Since Mother's was a pontifical order, her community was under the direct protection and care of the Vatican and not the local bishop. By its nature a Vatican visitation is an invasive affair. But the visitators were sensitive to the charged feelings in the house, and after a week, took their leave. In less than two months, the findings of the visitation would be at least partially revealed, as would the Vatican's strong medicine.

Angelica Exported

THROUGH THE CONTRETEMPS and dislocation in the monastery, all the charges and countercharges, Mother Angelica's mission flourished. Her physical effort was no longer required, only her spiritual participation was now necessary. She had indeed given God "foundations—new monasteries," even if it was not in the way she had initially envisioned.

Mother Dolores Marie, a determined, bespectacled nun, was the first of Angelica's daughters to become an abbess. At the end of 2002, the young sister left Hanceville to revive a dwindling community of Poor Clares in Portsmouth, Ohio. After trying for years to resuscitate the cloister there, Mother Dolores and four sisters decided to leave and accept an invitation from the diocese of Charlotte, North Carolina, in 2010. They were asked to build the first contemplative monastery in the diocese.

When Mother Dolores visited Charlotte, she instantly felt at home. It was Mother Angelica's guiding spirit of adventure and fidelity to God's will that propelled the nun onward.

"In all our lessons with Mother Angelica, she stressed that we would build mini-lights—houses where the Blessed Sacrament would be adored and loved all over the world. She told us that we were the future of the order, and as we grew we were supposed to be open to founding new foundations," Mother Dolores said. "She saw what needed to be done, and prepared us to be strong leaders of new communities."

By 2015, Mother Dolores had purchased 333 acres of land outside of Charlotte and was raising funds to build St. Joseph's Monastery and chapel, adjacent to a proposed seminary in the diocese. The sisters needed the additional space. Mother Dolores routinely received calls from women interested in joining their community, but the absence of rooms forbade the acceptance of any new sisters. It was a problem many communities would welcome. They continued raising money for the monastery, but before building commenced, a surprise requiring yet another move, awaited Mother Dolores and the five nuns in her care.

At this writing, Sister Grace Marie and her sisters temporarily reside in a local parish in San Antonio. They have secured the land to build St. Michael the Archangel Monastery and continue to fundraise. They routinely get inquiries from young women who feel called to the contemplative life. The buoyant group of sisters steadfastly believes that they will find the benefactors to complete their mission.

In France, Sister Antoinette and Sister Faustina Marie were among the nuns who reclaimed the first monastery of the Poor Clares of Perpetual Adoration in September of 2007. The esteemed monastery in Troyes, after a decade of being occupied by laypeople, was once again filled with Poor Clare nuns—seven to be exact. The sisters hailed from Cleveland, India, and, of course, Hanceville, Alabama. As providence would have it, Sister Antoinette was elected superior of the community in 2013. Though her creative leadership showed itself earlier.

The chapel of the Monastère Notre Dame des Anges was renovated in 2011. But the roof of the cloister still needed repair. When a building dates back to the fourteenth century, there's bound to be some leaks here and there. Sister Antoinette, channeling Mother Angelica's entrepreneurial spirit, set out to earn money for the roof as only she could. A concert violinist before coming to religious life, Sister Antoinette recorded a CD of Vivaldi's *Four Seasons* in the Cathedral of Troyes (the same cathedral where one of the founders of her order, Capuchin father Bonaventure Jean-Baptiste Heurlaut, was ordained). "You could say I was fiddling *for* the roof!" Sister Antoinette told the *National Catholic Register* in 2012.

No such roofing maladies afflicted Mother Angelica's Arizona nuns. In May of 2011, they dedicated a newly constructed chapel in the desert town of Tonapah, about an hour west of Phoenix. The medieval-style Our Lady of Solitude chapel bears architectural similarities to the order's shrine in Hanceville. But like her foundress, Sister Marie Andre is far from finished. The sisters have plans to build a forty-two-thousand-square-foot monastery complete with twenty-eight cells and a gift shop. The now autonomous monastery has four professed nuns, a postulant, and three women considering joining the community.

"We are thankful for what Reverend Mother handed on to us: her love for the Lord in the Blessed Sacrament. Seeing the chapel rise in the desert and knowing that He is adored there is so beautiful," Mother Marie Andre said. "I know it is what Mother would have wanted. I feel very much like her daughter, and we have followed her example of relying on His Providence. He is so generous."

Each new foundation has strived to preserve Mother's animating spirit and charism in the unique region entrusted to its spiritual care. The work of the "foundation sisters" conforms nicely with the following quote, which Mother Marie Andre recorded in a personal notebook and memorialized on the Desert Nuns website:

"A religious community which refuses to conform to the requirements of the times becomes unfaithful to its founder, for it will no longer be able to do the work confided to it. . . . A community keeps its youth if it is faithful to the spirit of its founder by striving to do things, not as they were done in the lifetime of the founder, but as the founder would do them if he were alive in our day."

Back in Hanceville, Mother Angelica was very much alive, and she continued to pray for the community in the midst of its travails. Mother Dolores Marie visited Mother during this time. When they were alone, she noticed that Angelica seemed preoccupied. "I said, 'Are you worried about anything?' because she knew what was happening in the community. She shook her head. She knew that God was in control and she was at peace and in total union," Mother Dolores remembered. "St. Francis thought because he had a clear vision of the community, that everyone could live it. But when the order expanded, it fell apart. Mother had the same flaw: she assumed that everyone had her vision and the same understanding that she had."

A former nun explained: "I don't think Mother is to blame for the problems—it's the self-love of the sisters who had to have their own way. Some were very ambitious, and no matter what Mother said, they would not listen to her. They had their own agenda. Some of them didn't get the greatest formation and never really learned to live in community."

Whatever the explanation, the Holy See had come up with its own remedies for dealing with the internal division at Our Lady of the Angels—remedies that would not be announced until a special honor was bestowed upon the foundress.

Roman Orders

ON OCTOBER 4, 2009, the feast of St. Francis, Mother Angelica was awarded the Pro Ecclesia et Pontifice ("For the Church and the Pope") Medal, the highest honor the pope can bestow on a religious or layman. Given her heroic efforts to spread and defend the Faith over many decades, she should have been accorded the honor years earlier. Mother more than qualified. After all, people as diverse as President Obama's surgeon general, Dr. Regina Benjamin, papal biographer George Weigel, broadcaster Father Michael Manning, and church benefactors around the world were all previous recipients of the honor. In Mother's case, the timing of the award was curious and surely deliberate.

The prestigious cross "for outstanding service and zeal" was formally awarded at the Vatican on July 20, 2009, according to the proclamation. But Bishop Robert Baker did not present the award to Mother until October 4, after a Vespers service at the Shrine of the Most Blessed Sacrament in Hanceville.

"The 'Pro Ecclesia et Pontifice Medal' is a significant acknowledgement by our Holy Father, of Mother's labors of love in support of our Church and of our Holy Father," the bishop said during his homily that day. Then he included this revealing addendum: "By giving awards, the Church is not saying people or institutions are perfect, but we are saying that Mother Angelica, through this

network, has made a significant contribution to the New
Evangelization heralded and promoted by recent Popes.
Mother Angelica's effort has been at the vanguard of the
New Evangelization and has had a great impact on our
world."

To the millions around the globe who had been
touched by her message and the broadcasts of EWTN,
no papal recognition of Mother's achievement was
necessary. And though she had more than earned the
honor, the timing of the presentation was likely a Roman
sleight of hand meant to distract from what was happening behind the scenes.

The results of the visitation were about to be unveiled:
In November of 2009 the Vatican would be importing
a new superior from outside the community. This seasoned nun would have dominion over the sisters, the
monastery, and all its affairs. Mother would be relieved
of her duties as abbess, and both Sisters Margaret Mary
and Catherine were to leave the house immediately for
at least a two-year sabbatical.

Our Lady of the Angels Monastery in a formal statement announced yet another "honor" the Church had
conferred upon Mother, along with other telling details
on November 23, 2009:

> On October 15, the feast of another eminent
> foundress, St. Teresa of Avila, Reverend Mother
> Angelica received a second major honor from

the Holy See, this time for her long and devoted guidance of the Poor Clare Nuns of Perpetual Adoration at Our Lady of the Angels Monastery: she was appointed Abbess Emerita for Life. Bishop Baker came to present her with the award in a private ceremony within the monastic enclosure at which Mother Angelica herself was able to be present in person. This reward for her labors not only recognizes her past work for her beloved monastic community but also entrusts to her for life a profound responsibility for the community's innermost wellbeing and growth in holiness. This task she has already begun through her prayer and suffering; she will continue to carry it out faithfully for the rest of her life on earth and, we have no doubt, into eternity. The monastery will thus never be without her Mother's love. At the same time, Mother has been released from responsibility for the day-to-day administration of the monastery.

Recognizing the faithful and selfless service rendered to the community by Sister Mary Catherine and Sister Margaret Mary as Reverend Mother's vicars during these past years, the Church has also granted both of them some sabbatical time away from the monastery for their own personal spiritual refreshment and renewal.

The community has thus begun a new and

exciting phase in our history under the guidance of the Holy Spirit. We have undertaken a lengthy period of spiritual renewal as we prepare to elect a new abbess. Two Sisters have been sent from other monasteries to assist us in our exploration of what it means for us today to be Poor Clares of Perpetual Adoration who are both heirs of Mother Angelica and faithful bearers of our tradition into the future. We are grateful for this opportunity, and we ask your prayers that we may enter into it with the wholehearted obedience to the Lord we and the world around us have always witnessed in Mother Angelica.

When Bishop Baker informed Sister Catherine and Sister Margaret Mary that they had both been instructed to leave the monastery, they were naturally disoriented. Uncertain of their next steps, the two nuns hastily prepared to depart the monastery they had long called home.

"They were two women who had different ideas about things—but not really," Sister Grace Marie opined. "They both loved Mother deeply."

Mother's successive Church honors helped camouflage the sweeping changes being imposed on the monastery and kept the story out of the media. Deacon Bill Steltemeier, who received the Pro Ecclesia et Pontifice award along with Mother, found himself in a similar position. Just months before the announcement of the papal honor, Steltemeier, who had been instrumental in helping Angelica launch the network and assumed power following her retirement, had his responsibilities shifted. Due to declining health and managerial over-reach, Steltemeier was made honorary chairman of the board at EWTN. Though he would no longer exercise any power within the organization he would live out his days as close to Mother Angelica as any layman could —in his residence just outside the monastery gates.

A Benedictine nun from Virginia Dale, Colorado, Sister Genevieve Glen, became the new superior of Our Lady of the Angels Monastery in November of 2009. With her arrival the two former vicars left the enclosure.

At the suggestion of Bishop Baker, Sister Catherine went to Rome to pursue studies at the Angelicum, the Pontifical University of St. Thomas Aquinas. While there, the nun felt called to begin a new order. At the end of her sabbatical period, Catherine was informed that she was welcome to remain a Poor Clare of Perpetual Adoration with financial support from the community but could not return to Our Lady of the Angels Monastery. Not wanting to confuse the public by wearing the Poor Clare habit out in the world, and feeling an internal prompting to establish a new religious order, she asked to be released from her vows in 2011. Catherine would instantly take private vows in Italy.

At the invitation of Bishop Luigi Negri of the diocese of San Marino-Montefeltro on the northeastern Italian coast, Sister Catherine founded a new community. Wearing a white habit, she now goes by the name Mother Gabrielle Marie, the superior of the Benedictine Daughters of the Divine Will.

"I was thirty-three when I entered Our Lady of the Angels, and I was there for thirty-three years," Mother Gabrielle Marie told me at the time of her departure. "Now I'm sixty-six years old, having trouble learning the language, but when God asks me to do something, I have to do it."

As of this writing the Benedictine Daughters of the Divine Will have four professed sisters and seventeen women from Italy and America interested in joining the group.

"The order has Mother Angelica's spirit," Mother Gabrielle Marie enthused. "We have a lot of joy and peace. There is no criticism. It is a house of charity." The Benedictine Daughters practice Eucharistic adoration, study the writings of Luisa Piccarreta, and are devoted to God's will. They are hoping to collect the necessary funds to renovate the Convent of Sant'Igne, a thirteenth-century Italian cloister reputedly built by St. Francis of Assisi.

Sister Margaret Mary eventually embraced her Carmelite yearnings. No longer a resident of Our Lady of the Angels Monastery, she now wears a Carmelite habit and is attached to a group of Carmelite monks in Wyoming.

She interacts with the monks and occasionally ventures into public, though she technically lives as a hermit.

Amid all the departures and changes taking place outside her cell, Mother Angelica maintained a quiet vigil, sleeping for longer periods of the day. There were, however, still days of not only lucidity, but clear communication. On February 21, 2010, a senior sister set a hot tea before Mother and began to gently chat with the foundress. "Do you think the Divine Child is going to take you soon, or heal you?" the nun impetuously asked. Mother considered the question for a long while.

"I don't want to live," Angelica declared gravely. "I owe Him much." Stirring her tea, lost in thought, she corrected herself. "I owe Him a lot."

Later the sisters handed Mother one of the Baby Jesus statues that dotted the bureaus and side tables of her room. As she caressed the image of the Divine Child, she continued to share her inner thoughts. "For the people," she said. "For the people." Confined to her room, in protracted silence and suffering, Mother still had an acute awareness of what this last period of her life was about. The sisters interpreted Mother's statements to mean that she had a personal desire to die—to be with Him—but she felt she owed the Lord a great deal and therefore would continue to suffer "for the people." Presumably the spiritual effects of that suffering would extend to those nearest her, those who now needed Mother's intercession as never before.

Outside Mother's cell at the monastery, additional sisters were asked to leave the house, and on December 1, 2010, one nun left with no prompting at all. Ninety-one-year-old Sister Bernadette, who had spent twenty-nine of her sixty years of religious life at the Alabama monastery, went to her reward. It was another blow to the sisters left behind. Soon the extern nuns (who lived outside the cloister) were disbanded, and the extern sisters sent home. At the time of the elections thirty-nine sisters filled the Hanceville cells, but by 2011, only eighteen nuns (not counting the two outside superiors) remained under the monastery roof.

Owing to a live Vespers service broadcast by EWTN each Sunday from the monastery, questions soon arose about the "missing nuns." Our Lady of the Angels Monastery eventually posted this explanation on their website:

> We continue to receive queries from EWTN viewers about the size of the monastic community. The community is definitely smaller than it was when the rosary programs were taped. We are now 20 Sisters. There are two reasons for this downsizing, besides the deaths of two of our beloved seniors. First, the community had reached its maximum of 45. That number, all the monastery could accommodate, proved to be too large for us to sustain the kind of familial community life Mother Angelica desired. We were also forced to turn away all applicants.

When that happy moment comes in the life of a monastery, it is traditional for the community to make new foundations to carry the charism into other places. This house did that in three ways: we sent nuns to make new foundations in Arizona (now in Tonopah) and San Antonio; we sent nuns to assist another PCPA monastery whose community was dwindling and aging; and we sent nuns to take part in an order-wide project to revive and preserve the mother house in Troyes, France. Those nuns all appear on the rosary tapes but are now serving Jesus in the Blessed Sacrament in new places. Secondly, we began a stronger screening program for applicants. The previous practice of accepting almost all comers had filled the building, but it had also led to many departures as young women without vocations entered, stayed for a while, and then left again, thus creating an atmosphere of instability that is not healthy for a cloistered contemplative monastery. The Lord continues to send us good vocations, for which we are deeply grateful, but they are entering in smaller numbers and a much larger percentage are persevering. Besides this intentional reduction in size, EWTN viewers should be aware that you do not see the entire community at Benediction. One Sister is always with Mother Angelica. And the soprano section of the choir is not visible because of camera angles. We're there, but you can't see us!

Regardless of the internal quarrels, the comings and goings at the monastery, the last line of that statement underscores what the contemplative life is really about—a mission often ignored by those in the larger world. Day in and day out, as we recreate, raise our families, make our deadlines, run from activity to activity, and even as we sleep, there are sacrificial souls praying in our stead. In monasteries and convents all over the world, religious like those at Our Lady of the Angels Monastery intercede for others, offering God praise and thanksgiving when the rest of the world forgets. Whether we think of them or not, they're there, but you can't see them. No matter the fairly minor disagreements that may have shaken the house for a time, the sisters were always unified in their mission and the importance of their life. The fruits of their prayers and sacrifices are abundant and the spiritual stakes much higher than they may seem at first glance. Nothing less than the salvation of souls, hope, and enduring love hang in the balance.

On April 27, 2011, sirens blared out their warnings in Hanceville, Cullman, and all over central Alabama. Menacing storm clouds gathered over the monastery of Our Lady of the Angels, and weather reports warned of tornadoes. Local weathermen urged people in the emergency zones to retreat to bathrooms in the center of their home or to basements. The sisters moved Mother Angelica to a rolling bed and transported her to a monastery parlor with no windows. It was one of the few times in years that she had vacated her room. And though the sisters were frightened, Mother actually enjoyed the experience. She was cheerful and buoyed by the excitement. When the power failed, some of the nuns were alarmed. But not Mother. In fact, the sisters told me that she drifted off to a contented sleep.

A string of tornadoes narrowly dodged Our Lady of the Angels Monastery but ravaged the nearby city of Cullman, killing two in town and claiming the lives of more than two hundred people in Alabama. The sisters thanked God for the protection of their house and begged His mercy for those who had lost homes, businesses, and loved ones.

Like their neighbors, the remaining nuns at Our Lady of the Angels had reconstruction of a different sort on their minds. They would be called to assess their current state, take deliberate steps to restore the unity Mother had always expected of them, and lay a spiritual foundation for growth into the future.

Continuing Duties

FOR MOTHER, LONG days stretched into weeks, months, and years. They were quiet, sleepy years. During meals and baths Angelica would offer the sisters fleeting access to the thoughts that were hers alone. "You don't know how hard it is not to be able to communicate," she told the nuns one day, with no prompting. It was a hard cross, especially for one with a well-exercised gift of communication.

But the silence was part of God's mysterious plan for Mother and a boon to her continuing work. There is a section of the Rite of the Anointing of the Sick, a sacrament that Mother received many times during her confinement, which reads: "Restore her, in your mercy, to full health of body and soul, so that having recovered by your goodness, she may take up her former duties." But Mother's "duties" never ceased. In fact, one could argue that the ability to execute her duties increased during her quiet years. Mother Marie Andre, the superior of the Phoenix monastery, put it this way in an interview in 2013:

> The Lord is so mysterious and ironic. Here she was for so many years *the voice*—such a gift. And it was understandable for people to think that until the day she died she would keep speaking. But Mother's like John the Baptist; he was the voice pronouncing the word. Then when he was imprisoned, he was in silence, darkness, totally hidden. He was in communion with the Lord. And that's what it's all about: the person and the Lord.
>
> Mother is more powerful saving souls now than she was when she was on air. She is a contemplative nun and her work occurs in silence—it is a hidden

life. The Lord has taken her back to the roots of her religious life. She will have a high place in heaven because of this time when she is doing her purgatory. The world thinks that when you are a celebrity on TV, that is where you do your greatest work. But I don't think that's true. She is now bedridden, her body is atrophied and she has to rely on others. What has happened for more than ten years has been her purification. How many people have been saved because of her sufferings? . . .

We may never know. Contemplatives rarely get to glimpse the good their prayers have produced. But as Mother's biographer I have been the recipient of hundreds of letters, testimonials from people whose lives have been renewed and forever altered by Mother Angelica's words or example. Each provides us with evidence of her wide appeal and spiritual influence. They also speak to the unseen power of Angelica's last years of silent suffering. What follows is but a smattering of the communications received from countless people who have experienced profound changes in their lives during Mother's active and hidden years, but mostly from this hidden period. I have elected to publish these stories with as little editing as possible, so that these members of Mother's extended "family" can speak for themselves.

Most of these people first encountered her on

television—and not always happily. So many of the letters I have received over the years start with complaints about first viewings of *Mother Angelica Live*. Usually fixated on the externals, these first-time viewers gripe: "I couldn't stand her scratchy voice," and "it was like nails on a chalkboard." But whether flipping through the channels with loved ones or sitting alone in a hotel room searching for porn (as one man revealed), they all found the same "spunky nun." And, more important, they came back to listen to her again and again.

Charlene Allison Briggs was one of those who didn't care for Mother's voice at first. Briggs captured the common reaction to repeated viewings of the live show when she wrote:

> Her voice, much to my surprise, was not so grating; it had become inviting—she was talking to my heart. In 2005, I realized I was listening to my favorite "voice" on TV—Mother Angelica. I so loved her re-aired shows and in my opinion she won "Best in Comedy," "Best in Drama," and "Best in Places of My Heart." Now here it is 2012. I pray the rosary with Mother, I listen to her reruns and yes, I keep her between my gas and electric bills. I have no reason to listen to the TV show called "The Voice," because I have been listening to the original "voice" for years and have been touched by the Holy Spirit for doing so.

Due to the reach of her cable network, Mother was able to touch people in various states of life, some in unimaginable circumstances. A surprising number of her viewers knew nothing about Catholicism or even Christianity. James Walden, who shared his story with me, is one such person:

> When I lived in New York City in 2005, I was effectively a very bitter atheist with no positive experience of religion, nor of God. I watched at first with detached fascination and then a deep emotional profundity the news of Pope John Paul II's death. For an entire day I sat wrapped in a blanket, tears streaming down my face in grief for the loss of a man I'd never known nor cared about. But his powerful testimony in frailty and illness, his courage in the face of death, and his witness to the truths of God moved me and opened my heart. . . . I had found EWTN and through Mother's ministry, I was able to be educated and inspired in a dark time in my life when I had no one to share my spiritual agonies with, no one to take my concerns to, no one to talk with about the intellectual and historical realities of Christ in His Church. I watched daily for two years, absorbing wisdom and knowledge and grace through an otherwise lonely conversion. Then one day I turned off the television, put on my hat, took up

my stick and walked to the local Catholic Church.
I asked for Baptism. I asked for acceptance into
God's people. As Mother's apostolate implicitly
foretold, they welcomed me and I found that
I had come to more than just faith; I had come
home . . . though Mother Angelica does not know
me, and did not begin her apostolate with me in
mind, she has lived out her vocation in me.

One man, David Gonzales, lost to his addiction,
found an unexpected way back to sobriety and life.
Mother Angelica showed him the way:

Where do I start? I drank and took drugs for 47
years. 3 years ago, I was at the bottom and I prayed
to God to help me surrender all my bad habits, but
it was hard. I had never heard of EWTN. As I was
struggling one day, I started scanning through the
TV channels and there is Mother Angelica, what
a gift from God. I am happy to tell you that I am
free of alcohol, and drugs. It's been three years
now, and I have never experienced life this way.
From the first time I started watching her I have
looked forward to her program. My Granddaughter
used to ask me, "Why are you watching church all
day?" My response was, "Do you want me to drink
again?" I try to make Mass everyday, I pray my
Rosarie [sic] everyday. I also learned how to read

Scripture by listening to Mother Angelica. Excuse my spelling I only went to the 9th grade. In one of her programs, Mother told me, "God wasn't looking for education. . . ." May God bless Her and I look foreweard [sic] to chatting with Her in Heaven. Amen!

Joseph Escarsiga wrote this moving letter about his encounter with Mother. He found her during a very dark period in his life:

I love you Mother, and I pray for you as often as I can because when I was lost in drug addiction and a life of rampant criminality, when I thought that there was no love for me, you pointed me to the Light. I am 40 years old praise be to God Almighty for allowing me to make it this far. I am a father of 2 wonderful little girls . . . they're the apple of my eye! I am married to the most loving woman, so giving and so patient, but it would all be just a dream if not for your help . . . through your program on EWTN I have been able to understand my life and my purpose, to love and to know God, and was able to survive and escape a lifetime of organized crime and drugs and return to my God and Your God, prodigal son that I was. . . . I struggle daily through many things, but He has been my Bulwark, my Refuge. . . .

Thank you for your life's work and know that I am but one of many who through your love for Christ and His Church have been and continue to be touched to the core, to the very soul. May God Bless you Mother and the entire work of your hands. . . . Love, Joseph

Those in dire straits, in the midst of a life crisis, often tell the most dramatic of stories. In their moment of despair, providentially, Mother was always present for them. This is from Carolyn Harrison. She like so many others found Mother years after the nun had retired from television, once speech had all but abandoned her:

Five years ago at age 57, I was in a fetal position on my 92 year old mother's couch. Earlier that day, quite by accident (?), I discovered my husband had been having an affair in our home while I was away on business. I came home a day early to find a pajama top with a picture of Buddha on it. The pajama top had been smoothed carefully over my pillow on my side of the marital bed. I was in shock and could barely speak for several minutes. My skin felt on fire.

By the grace of God, I was able to drive to my mother's home only to collapse on her couch, a shattered person. As the day passed into night,

I kept changing pillows as often as I changed television channels, sobbing uncontrollably.

Exhausted and unable to sleep, I once again began to mindlessly surf the channels when I landed on EWTN, what stopped me hitting the button again was seeing Mother Angelica in her habit. My soul recognized she was a nun and I immediately felt comfort. Mother was talking about fidelity to God and to each other and what was right and wrong in life.

I was active in the Episcopal Church when I discovered the infidelity. I had always felt appreciation for the Catholic Church, but, like most Protestants, did not fully understand it. However, I wholeheartedly agreed with what Mother Angelica was saying about truth, right and wrong.

Mother Angelica talked about what it meant to be honest and courageous and encouraged viewers to stand firm for what was right. STAND FIRM FOR WHAT WAS RIGHT. Those words started my healing. There is a beautiful Dominican Cloister Monastery in the Hollywood Hills near my home. I started attending Mass five years ago at the Monastery going up for a blessing. . . . On October 4, 2011, the Feast Day of Saint Francis of Assisi, I received my first Holy Communion in the Roman Catholic Church.

I thank God for Mother Angelica's devotion to fidelity and for wearing the habit. It was the nun's habit that calmed my heart long enough so that my mind could capture the words of fidelity I desperately needed to hear.

From her bed in Our Lady of the Angels Monastery, Mother's timing remained impeccable—and she was always there. Angelica had a particular resonance with those battling addictions, the lost, and the hurting. Given her personal background, Mother developed a tender heart for such people, as Mary Berman can attest:

I was a successful professional person, but slowly fell into the depths of alcoholism. I was in total denial of the existence of any higher power, much less the Lord Jesus Christ. As years went by, along with several other additional husbands and divorces, I finally met a Jewish man whom I married. Seventeen years later he died in my arms. I fell deeper into the throes of alcohol, drugs, and smoking. . . . The death of my husband gave me an excuse to begin those old habits (vices) again. I was angry at God . . . killing myself slowly with alcohol and pills. I didn't even care if I woke up again. . . .

I knew I needed to change. I longed for

sobriety. I had reached a bottom . . . friends and family didn't want to be around me. . . . I was very lonely and depressed when one Tuesday evening I was channel surfing, and there was THAT NUN! I couldn't take my eyes off of her, and I wanted to listen to what she had to say. Of all things, that evening a woman called in who was an alcoholic—she couldn't stop drinking. Mother gave her advice like only Mother can. I could relate so much. She paused and called everyone to prayer for the alcoholic woman. It was then that I knew that Mother was praying for me too. I bowed my head and prayed with Mother Angelica. I do not believe it was an accident that I happened to turn to EWTN that night.

I have been sober now for nearly 3 years. I have gone through RCIA and am now a Catholic. I have had 4 nullifications of previous marriages.

An amusing incident happened last year when I was cleaning my bedroom closet at my parents' home. I found a copy of *Mother Angelica's Answers Not Promises* which I had purchased 30 years ago and had forgotten about. I smiled and said to myself, "You've always been there, haven't you!?!"

Mother Angelica appeared in the lives of some people at the end of their struggle, when it mattered most. This affecting letter was written by Juliana Mammana:

Our daughter Julia was diagnosed with lung cancer and came to live with us here in Camarillo so she could get her treatments at the Ventura County Hospital.

Julia struggled with alcohol and drug addictions and was also bi-polar. It was a challenging time, but also a blessing. . . . She worried that God wasn't going to forgive her for the life she had led, and that was when Mother Angelica's words came to mind: "It's an insult to God when you think your sins are greater than His Mercy." It brought her some consolation. Julia passed away at the end of August 2011 with the knowledge that her family forgave her, and that God in His Mercy would do the same.

Mother's words had powerful effects. Jim Nicholson shared this encounter with Mother Angelica—one he credits with his conversion to the Catholic faith and for leading him to discover the true purpose of his life:

On one of her shows on purgatory—and this affected me more deeply than anything I had ever heard a religious or anyone say at any time ever—Mother said, "I would spend purgatory for every one of you if you would just say yes to God." Raymond, she had me in tears. I decided right there and then . . . that there is more to life

than just living from day to day, and not really
wondering what kind of plan God had for me. . . .
I decided I would no longer allow anyone or any
situation in life to deter me from trying to walk
along with God on the path He set for me, no
matter what earthly cost I may have to pay. And I
try to live this moment to moment.

Those with disabilities were especially attentive to
Angelica's message. After all, Mother was a woman beset
by physical limitations who with faith and gumption defied the odds and achieved great things. Rita Smithson
could relate. She found Mother Angelica long after the
nun had fallen silent, aside from televised reruns that
continued to air:

I did not know Mother Angelica existed until April
2010. That was the month I was diagnosed with
Multiple Sclerosis. I was no longer able to return to
work. So one day, out of boredom I started channel
surfing. I came across this program with this older
nun sitting and describing her difficulty with
walking and wearing braces on her legs. This nun
immediately grabbed my full attention as I sat there
glued to her every word. She had also mentioned
how she hated nuns and she began to laugh that
she now was one herself. When she described the
beauty of reconciliation for those that have been

away from the Church, she said, "If I were you I would be beating the door down. DON'T WAIT. You don't know when he will say, 'COME.'" She held up her hand and made a motion with her fingers as the signal to come. After hearing her on this program, I said to myself, "Who is this wonderful nun?" Mother Angelica and I have a lot in common. I have difficulty walking; we share a birth name, Rita; and recalling my Catholic school days—I was not happy with nuns either. But most of all she inspired me to come home. I have now returned to Mass on a regular basis. After being away for a long period of time I made my general confession with a wonderful priest at my local parish. I wished I could have called Mother Angelica to share the joy of my reconciliation experience with her. If it wasn't for her, I shudder to think of the consequences. I wished I had known of her sooner in my life. I pray that the joy of the Lord is her strength, until He says, "Mother, COME."

Lorrie Benemerito also found consoling guidance in Mother's words during a health crisis. The nun's words became ever more important as time went on. This letter was addressed to Mother and me in March of 2012:

When I first had found my cancerous breast lump, almost two years ago, my first thought was: "Don't think about all the painful scenarios that might come to pass, just live in the now." I was basing my thoughts upon what was engraved within the confines of my mind—a mind that held the words of Mother Angelica: "Live in the present moment." Great advice. I took it, and I applied it throughout this nearly two-year battle with breast cancer. Needless to say, it helped to soothe my soul, time and time again.

The second Mother Angelica teaching, and a most important one, is to offer up one's self, for another. This cancer journey of mine, as with many illnesses experienced in my 63 years on this planet, has afforded me many incredibly painful experiences. But it all has been gathered up, each and every time, and offered to the Father, thru Jesus. I know in my heart, that it all has been used—it all has become redemptive or has aided a "cause." . . .

Now that my cancer has spread to various places, including both of my lungs, I am at stage IV. Too weak to do Chemo, having one med as a possible aid to keep me alive a while longer, I will continue to practice these mental and spiritual "modes of living."

If I am enjoying a delicious, home-cooked dinner, or taking in a beautiful sky, I will live in that moment, and enjoy the food and the beauty!

And everyday, every moment of every difficulty, will continue to be offered-up.

Mother Angelica, I thank you for your words of wisdom and truth, and for weaving them into the tapestry of my life. I love you and I believe we will meet in Heaven, where neither one of we paisanos will even have a memory of our former earthly pain. We will only get to see the fruits of our "offerings up"!

A woman named Judy lost her son, Alan, in a car accident. In despair, she wrote to Mother Angelica. Angelica's personal response to the grieving woman was just the right mix of tough love and compassion that she needed at the time of Alan's passing.

In a letter Mother wrote on July 29, 1997, she reminded Judy that Jesus had conquered death. She counseled the woman to "face death and let it change you for the better." Then invoking the faith of the Virgin Mary who watched her son die horrifically before her, Mother Angelica writes, "We must imitate her. Through the terrifying darkness of this life, we must cling to the supernatural hope that was planted in our hearts at baptism . . . you cannot stop praying . . . as painful as it is to face death with God, how could you face it without Him? Trust Him and let Him help you. He loves you."

Consolation was only part of what Mother gave her viewers. Often it took many years for her effect upon them to be felt. But it would leave a profound mark. These quiet, less dramatic stories are as important as any of the more heartrending ones.

Patricia E. wrote:

> It is no exaggeration to say that Mother Angelica has meant the difference between life and death to our family. I can't remember the first time I accidently turned on EWTN around 1991, and was amused to find a feisty, intelligent and humorous nun, not unlike nuns who had taught me in grade school: talking, laughing and speaking the truth. It was that last one, speaking the truth, that got me. It was a breath of fresh air, light in the darkness. . . . Over time, I realized I was not living my faith, I thought I was Catholic, but in reality, I was far, far from God. Mother taught me my Faith, gave me back all I had lost and even more. This was at a crucial time in my life, as a mother of three young children, when the world was telling me that three was enough! Thanks be to God for Mother Angelica! . . . My fourth child was born in 1992, the fifth in 1995, a sixth in 1997. . . . Other little ones who went to heaven before they could be born as well. Through Mother's teaching us our Faith, we were able to pass it on to our children as they grew and became parents themselves. We now have eight grandchildren and counting. Eternal

lives! . . . May God reward Mother Angelica for her faithfulness and trust. (And grant her a jewel in her crown for each member of our family!!!)

Like many of us, Lisa Krenik of Woodland, Texas, was a procrastinator. She had felt inspired to write a book decades earlier. But it wasn't until she came across a *Mother Angelica Live* rerun in 2010 that Lisa got moving:

"Just Begin!" These two simple words became the best and most "life changing" advice I ever received from our dear Mother Angelica. I had tuned in to EWTN one weekday morning in the fall of 2010 and was listening to one of her Mother Angelica Live shows originally broadcasted many years ago. (Mother Angelica's wise advice is never dated . . . it is timeless!)

A young woman had called in to ask Mother the following question: "If you feel like you are being called to do something, how do you know this is coming from God and not from some other source?" Mother's response:

"If you feel you are being called to do something, *just begin* sweetheart. If this is from God, the doors will then begin to open for you to continue." This was just the answer and advice I needed to hear from Mother.

For close to 25 years, I had had the feeling that I should write a children's book. Well the years quickly went by. I married, . . . was constantly traveling with my job, and became very busy caring for elderly family. . . . However, the thought that I was supposed to write this children's story never left me. In fact, it "haunted" me!

Hearing Mother's words . . . "Just begin" . . . was the right encouragement at the right time for me! Right then and there, I made a vow to myself to "just begin" writing this children's story. My original short story idea now has evolved into a trilogy of sorts. Some days I would write for 9 hours straight. Some days I became so engrossed in my project . . . it would be 4:00 p.m., and I would still be in my pajamas! . . . My children's story may or may not be published one day, but even so, this process of writing it has truly blessed me and healed me . . . and the habit of "just beginning" is now helping me in many other areas of my life as well!

This is how she touched people most often, in the midst of their daily lives—when they craved a word of guidance or correction. A cardiac technician living in Saudi Arabia wrote that he found Mother on satellite television one afternoon. Through her teaching, he learned to pray the rosary and rediscovered his Catholicism. When he was pressured by others to abandon his faith, the man claims that his brush with Mother kept him "from becoming a Muslim." Today, still living in Saudi Arabia, he secretly prays a tiny rosary he carries in his hand on the bus to work each day. He asked me to suppress his name for fear of reprisals.

Henry Binghi was a stay-at-home father working in his kitchen when he received a "call" from Mother Angelica that would take him down a very different path:

> I was about midway through a pile of dishes when my TV in the living room came on all by itself. I repeat, I am washing the dishes in the kitchen, the kids were at school, my wife was at work and the TV comes on all by itself. As I turned around to see what was happening, I see Mother Angelica on the screen. The camera comes in with a close up shot and she begins to point, and then the words out of her mouth were, "God is calling you." It was as if she was talking to ME! That was what I would call a "wow" moment. . . . I got a chuckle at first, but then as my life began to take shape, we were all growing closer to our Lord. I can reflect back and see that God was calling me. . . . Months later the phone rings. My Pastor asked me to interview for the position as Director of Religious Education. Yet another wow moment . . . I took the job. By first hearing Mother

Angelica pop up on the TV that day and speak those words, I turned and started following the path back to practicing our wonderful Catholic faith!

Others, like Ken Toohill, credit Mother with helping them salvage a personal relationship—in this case a marriage:

How has Mother Angelica touched my life? Oh boy!!!

Here is the short of it: my wife and I went through a separation and civil divorce beginning ten years ago. Our marriage (1986) was never annulled—so we are still married in the church. Thirty years ago this Valentines Day was our first date and we are going out to dinner and a movie tomorrow on THIS Valentines Day, as we are working to rebuild our marriage.

In 2001 I moved out due to her abuse toward me. At that time I found EWTN and began listening to Mother Angelica. Because of Mother I began praying for Debra almost daily. Three years ago Debra gave me a tearful apology. This past November she was diagnosed with a brain tumor requiring immediate surgery. I spent hours with her during the time of her brain surgery, and introduced her to EWTN, Mother Angelica and the nuns from OLAM. Debra and I said the rosary with Mother during her hospital stay. She fell in love with Mother.

Today Debra has no cancer, returned to work, and has been totally healed in numerous ways. She has never felt better.

Tomorrow I'm announcing my renewed relationship with Debra to friends and family. We still have separate homes but are prayerfully moving forward one step at a time. How is that for a happy Mother Angelica story?

Pat Leszkowicz was diagnosed with multiple sclerosis in 1993. In time she grew despondent and obsessed about the future. Then she came across Mother Angelica:

> Outwardly I seemed normal; I could walk, see, talk and move normally, but inside I was so depressed that I was barely functioning. I felt my life had ended; I had no future except total paralysis and dependence. . . . Days came and went; I kept busy with housework, laundry, and cooking but inside I was empty; no joy or happy anticipation.
>
> One bleak morning, as I was flipping through the TV channels, I found a little nun looking back at me. She was dressed in real nun clothes. I stopped changing channels because something felt so safe and comforting about her. I do not

remember what she was saying exactly in the beginning but I kept listening and feeling better.

The nun, who I learned later was Mother Angelica, was answering questions that people were phoning in. Then came the "miracle."

A woman called and said she had Multiple Sclerosis and she was upset because her children kept telling her to "get out of the house, find something to do. Don't just stay home." And Mother Angelica said, "What is wrong with staying home and doing those things? You do what you can; your cleaning and preparing the home and doing such things are good."

That made me realize, if it came to that, if all I could do was stay home, then it would be all right . . . maybe that is what God is asking of me.

I am thankful to God for sending that little nun to reach the whole world through her TV station. Mother Angelica has given me so much hope and faith that I cannot express my gratitude and thankfulness.

Others were thankful for the personal encounters they had with Mother when she was still active. Simple acts observed, or words shared, enriched their lives for the better, as the following letters demonstrate.

Father Michael Galea, a priest from Baton Rouge,

Louisiana, recalls Mother visiting his diocese in the early 1980s shortly before she founded EWTN:

> She was trying to figure out what kind of television studio she wanted and how big it would be. She was shown some of the local stations. When I had the privilege to meet her in person that evening, she mentioned that she liked one of the stations that she had seen, and of course I agreed with her. I told her that that specific TV station would be big enough for her. She turned around and looked me in the eyes and told me, "Father, never cheat God. That station serves as a beginning."
>
> I got my lesson, and she received my donation for her project! Every time I had to ask any of my congregations for money, I would always use that line of Mother's: "Never cheat God, whatever we are doing is just the beginning."

Pamela Riess-Ogurko, a Lutheran, experienced Mother's touch through an ailing friend. Pamela went to Veterans' Stadium in Long Beach, California, in the early 1990s to hear Mother Angelica speak:

> I attended the event with two long-time Catholic friends, Peggy Singleton and George Vieira. George had been diagnosed with a rare, progressive brain disorder that affected his speech

and ability to walk. . . . As Mother concluded her talk, George expressed his desire to meet her. She was already being led to her transportation when Peggy and I began to frantically call out to her. Mother Angelica looked up at us and waved. We yelled, "Please wait!" Then we proceeded to virtually drag George down the steps to the field below. I remember his legs appeared to be straight out behind him and his toes were leaving tracks in the dirt. Finally, we made it to Mother's side and she kindly placed her hands on George's head and prayed for him. George later said that he saw bright flashes of light when Mother touched him. Mother Angelica then placed her hands on both Peggy and me. Raymond, Mother truly touched our lives that day, and although George didn't receive a physical healing, his life greatly improved. His faith grew to where we looked upon him as a living saint. He died in January at 79. He often said that after Mother's blessing he came to realize that his disability is what made his faith so strong. I myself became a full-fledged Catholic with the support of Peggy and George and the example of Mother Angelica's dedication to Jesus.

John P. Van der Zalm wrote to share the story of his personal meeting with Mother at the Birmingham monastery in early 1992. John and his wife had driven all the way down from Ontario. Spying Mother Angelica, they excitedly ran up to inform her of their arduous trek. "Mother, unimpressed by our driving feat, put her arms around us and said, 'Why don't you go into the Chapel and first say Hi to Jesus and then we can talk later.'" Van der Zalm continued, "She always had her priorities right and her 'subtle' way of delivery was unequalled."

Linda Gaspers had a quieter, but no less profound visit with Mother in 2008, after faithfully watching the nun on television for years and praying with her nightly. In this letter to Mother Angelica she recounts her fervent prayer:

> that if I ever got the chance to come to visit the Shrine [in Hanceville], I would be able to see you in person, hug you, or at least touch your hand and tell you, "Thanks for your 'Yes' to God's Will, and for being His instrument in bringing us the invaluable gift of EWTN!!!"
>
> Well, my prayers were truly answered on Jan. 28, 2008 as my son, Matthew, and I were in the parlor holding your hand and looking into your eyes of love. I was able, through tears in my eyes, to thank you and tell you how much you mean to me and those around the world that you have touched very deeply. I feel I have touched the hands of one who will one day be a saint! In your eyes, I could see and feel the presence of God. . . .

You were not able to speak at that time, but no words were needed. I thank God over and over for allowing this miracle to happen when everyone said, "You won't be able to see Mother." That miracle certainly strengthened my faith in God!

I often ask God to make me as strong, persevering, and faithful to Him as you have taught us to be through your life, Mother. As you told us, "He never said it was going to be easy, but He did say that He will be there to help us if only we ask."

This idea was not lost on Ken Crawford. He sent me the following brief, insightful letter, which perfectly captured the heart of Mother's spirituality and the focus of her life during her hidden years:

Mother Angelica's biggest gift to me is her suffering.

Sounds crazy, doesn't it? I've got an MS-like disease with many complications. Stuck in a wheelchair with pain, weakness, yadda yadda . . . Mother has shown me that suffering is a noble, generous vocation.

I'll never forget the day she and the nuns prayed a Rosary live on EWTN. She kept struggling, kept making mistakes (One decade had twelve "Hail Mary's"). We struggled with her, we prayed with her, we cried with her. Just as we watched JP II agonize to share his last words with us, we helped Mother drag each word from her heart.

No more live EWTN broadcasts—she is now doing what she has always wanted to do. She spends hours praying and adoring Jesus in the silence of her heart.

During the last years, Mother had a regular bed companion: a bloated tabby named Mikey could often be spied nestling near her feet. Owing to Mother's asthma, she could never previously have cats anywhere near her. But following her stroke, Mother's asthma simply vanished, and she regularly had not one but two feline companions at any time. She seemed to enjoy their company. The cats were cuddly, asked nothing of her, and were exceedingly quiet.

Sometimes when I visited Mother in her room she would be sparkling and alert. On one occasion, I decided to read her a parcel of letters from people who had been changed by her words or example, including many of the letters quoted above. Mother was eating bananas and ice cream at the time, happily consuming each spoonful offered by Sister Gabriel. At the conclusion of every letter, I would scan the next few notes, trying to locate the most interesting ones to share with her. My search apparently went on too long for Mother's taste. After several minutes, I glanced up and noticed her staring at me—hard. She dodged Sister Gabriel's full spoon and with some exasperation told me, "Go on." When I continued reading she once again accepted the ice cream.

She delighted in hearing these personal tales, smiling and more often than not tearing up at the stories of the many lives she had managed to transform. Every so often she would close her eyes and nod, as if in prayer. When she opened them again, fresh tears of thanksgiving would present themselves.

There were a couple of times when I observed an amusing phenomenon in Mother's room. Another visitor would enter the cell and instantaneously, Mother's eyelids would grow heavy. In seconds she was out. Dead asleep. After staring at the snoozing nun for some time, the visitor would express disappointment at having "missed her" and eventually, conceding defeat, leave the cell. Within moments, Mother's eyes would snap open, and seeing that the coast was clear, she would wink or emit a little chortle. She wasn't sleeping, just playing possum to avoid extended conversations with people she couldn't or didn't care to deal with at the time. It was her only means of escape.

Mother Angelica was often solemn in the later part of 2011. Yet during my visits I had a sense that between the groggy periods and the natural frustration, she still understood that God was using her in a powerful way. It made me think of something she once said: "The greatest days of my life were when I had braces and crutches. I felt I was a real witness then. And now I'm still a witness. . . . But the only thing that is important is, Am I loving God and growing holy every day?"

In her cell, Mother was still loving God, witnessing to the world, and imparting final lessons to those distant and very near.

CHAPTER 5

What Mothers Do

Here are my mother and my brothers! For whoever does the will of my Father in heaven is my brother, and sister, and mother.

—MATTHEW 12:49–50

THERE IS ONE question that I am bound to hear after any speech and certainly during a book signing. It has come up again and again for many years: "Raymond, tell us how you met Mother Angelica—and what she taught you, personally." In the past I have opted to dodge the question, preferring to highlight one of Mother's random teachings and leave it at that. When you spend so much of your life in public, there are some things you wish to keep to yourself. Still there are questions that never go away.

On the hour-long drive from Hanceville to

Birmingham after each of my last visits with Mother, I found myself returning to the second part of that familiar question: *What did she teach you?* And what of her wisdom and example do I hope to pass along to my children and others?

How we met is easier, so I'll start there.

In 1995, I was a Capitol Hill correspondent living in Washington, D.C. EWTN was not available on my cable system in the District, so I had no knowledge of its existence or of the nun who had founded it. One night, after a dinner party in Virginia, the host asked if I had ever seen Mother Angelica.

"Who?" I asked.

He laughed, darted across the room, and began rummaging through a cabinet beneath his TV. "You will not believe this nun!" he promised. Pulling a VHS tape out of the cabinet as if he had just unearthed a piece of the true cross, he jammed the cassette into the player with a subversive glee. Curious members of the dinner party settled in around the television.

"This is from a few years ago in Denver—at World Youth Day. You will not believe where this goes," the host promised those gathered.

Judging from the static as the program started, the video had been viewed many, many times. "Mother's Corner," the rather cheesy purple and white graphics read. Then three words popped up: "The Hidden Agenda." From my first glimpse of the old nun on screen, wearing a tan veil and a modern brown habit, I knew I had seen that face before. Being half Italian, I was familiar with what my mother's side of the family called *la faccia lunga*—a long-faced, ticked-off expression. This chubby nun was sporting a full-frontal *la faccia lunga*!

Her chin was tucked to her chest, a fist clenched over her heart. This paisana looked as if she was about to throw a left hook. Slowly, the old nun began spitting out words with a simmering intensity: "We've had a tremendous week, we've seen Catholicity in action, we've seen spirituality working. . . ." She was commenting from Denver's World Youth Day in August of 1993. A day earlier, EWTN had broadcast an outdoor Way of the Cross, where the role of Jesus had been played by a young woman. Mother Angelica was beside herself.

In the video, her eyes darted side to side, anger rising with each line. "The prayers were beautiful. But they depicted Our Lord as a woman— an abomination to the Eternal Father!" She then pointed her finger into the camera. "It was a statement and I'm going to make a statement also." For the next thirty minutes, Mother uncorked the rage she had been holding down for years, reflecting the feelings of so many Catholic faithful whose old devotions and traditional practices had been diminished, derided, or just stamped out. "I'm tired of your tricks. I'm tired of your deceit," Angelica fumed. She called out the organizers of the Way of the Cross, charging that they were part of a hidden agenda to embarrass

the pope and to advance the cause of female ordina-
tion. "You spread your errors to children and they don't
even know the Eucharist anymore . . . I'm so tired of
you, liberal Church in America." Her eyes moist with
emotion, she lashed out at those who had belittled the
simple faith of the masses. "You want to destroy, so you
plant this mime, this woman as Jesus. You can't stand
Catholicity."

Her impassioned, unscripted feverino was like the
emancipation proclamation for traditional Catholics—a
rallying cry for all of those who had ever been attacked for
doing the things they had been taught. "We are Roman
Catholics of a Latin rite, we are not Lefeverites, we are
not conservatives, we are merely Catholic!" Mother Angelica railed. "Don't call me rebellious. No. You are rebellious." These were fighting words—a line in the sand.
"I resent you pushing your anti-Catholic, ungodly ways
upon the masses of this country . . . I'll tell you and the
whole world, I intend to remain a Roman Catholic. I
intend to be faithful to the Holy Father and the Church
and I will not obey your disobedient ways. I've made
my statement, you've made yours. Maybe it's time you
go your own way. Live your lives. Live your falsehoods.
Live your lies. Leave us alone . . . It's time we say that. I
don't like your kind of religion. I don't like your ways. . . .
You have no right to destroy people's faith—the faith of
the children, the faith of the elderly—by these shenani-
gans."

At that Virginia house party, a roomful of people who had never seen the chubby nun from Birmingham began to cheer. She got the blood pumping. Here was a woman on fire, who in layman's terms laid out the crisis facing the Church and told all comers that she had had enough and was willing to fight for the true faith. It was exhilarating, from-the-gut television with no frills. Mother Angelica had left an impression on me long before I ever met her.

At the end of that year, Deal Hudson, editor of *Crisis* magazine, asked me to write a cover story on Mother Angelica for his journal. He knew I had a print background, and since I worked in television, he thought it would be a good fit. With that passionate clip from World Youth Day as my only frame of reference, I accepted the assignment and made plans to head to Birmingham, Alabama, at the end of January. I would interview some of the principals, tour the EWTN facility, and meet Mother Angelica in her office for a one-on-one sit-down before I left.

From the moment I laid eyes on her, it was as if we had known each other our whole lives. There was an instantaneous rapport and an ease that usually takes years to establish. Our shared Italian heritage certainly strengthened the affinity. I think she also liked that I was not worshipful around her, but outspoken and direct. Throughout the interview she answered phone calls from the monastery, chatted with visiting network vice presidents, and we even discussed some ideas for news programming at EWTN. Mother was distressed by what she had seen on Catholic and secular news outlets. She thought them to be "biased," shallow, and "cold." She wanted something different—an independent news source, committed to the search for truth, yet free from control by the bishops or any other entity. Mother spoke of the need for a "homey" newscast, one where the anchor "had compassion" and displayed "a very human touch." Following our interview, I sat in the studio audience for her live show and was to leave the next morning.

Before I departed for the airport I decided to tell Mother Angelica good-bye. We met in her monastery parlor.

"So what are you going to do in D.C.?" she asked, settling back in her chair.

"Well, I'm still covering the Capitol, and I have been talking to some cable networks about—"

Before I could finish, Mother laced her hands together and said, "Why don't you start a news operation for us?" This was the last thing I expected to hear—though it was intriguing. I bought myself some time by reminding her that I was recently married and had to discuss it with my wife. We agreed that I would consider her offer and touch base soon.

For Mother, "soon" was a matter of days.

One night in early February of 1996, my wife, Rebecca, and I were returning from a long, depressing congressional event. Having covered Capitol Hill for a number of years, I had grown increasingly impatient with the power lobbyists exercised in Congress and had little interest in covering the same debates with the same players year after year. On the drive home, poor Rebecca was treated to a protracted rant colorfully citing examples of the above. As we walked into the apartment, the phone rang. It was 10:15 p.m.

"Hello."

"Well . . . you ready to come down here?" a sprightly voice on the other end asked.

"Who is this?"

"Mother."

"This is not my mother. Who is this?"

"It's *Mother Angelica*. Is this Raymond?"

"Oh, Mother, I'm sorry I didn't realize . . ."

She started laughing and sprang her trap: "So are you ready to come down here?" Then the dramatic pause. "It'll be good for your soul."

Before I could even answer she said, "Bring your wife down. Come for a visit. I'll set everything up."

What are you supposed to say to an offer like that? Naturally, I agreed. Shortly after our visit, Michael Warsaw, the vice president of programming, came to D.C. to formally offer me the job of news director over a pasta dinner. Mother wasted little time.

I would be lying if I said that my early years at EWTN

(or even a few of the years that followed) were wall-to-wall sweetness and light. Reading my diaries from the period, I am struck by the tumult of those early days.

Coming from a background in the theater and having worked at professional broadcast and print outlets, I had a bit of culture shock when I started at EWTN. There were no scripts or teases going into commercial breaks. Lighting and sound were secondary considerations. Procedures and standards that had become routine for me were simply not part of the EWTN approach to television. Wanting to improve the quality of the broadcasts, I could be exacting in my attention to details related to my program, and probably a bit demanding. The lights needed readjustment. The music in the show's opening lacked drive. The editing was too languid. What I saw as constructive evaluations—a part of the "creative process"—were viewed by my coworkers at the time as offensive critiques. Mother interpreted the complaints she began receiving from a few employees as a sign that I "lacked humility." Thus began the first of many lessons she tried to pass on to me.

A Touch of Humility

DURING THE FIRST two years on the job Mother would routinely, and in front of others, call me out for lacking humility. One day as she passed me in an EWTN hallway, flanked by two executives, she announced, "If I can teach you a little humility you'll be the perfect news-man."

"We'll talk about it," I replied with a smile, as she proceeded down the hall.

The clinking of her crutches stopped. With some effort she spun around and came straight at me: "After I speak I'm used to other people saying nothing."

Not wanting to cause a scene, I thought it best to take her advice. But Mother had already read my face, which despite my best efforts, often tells a thousand tales. Her eyes narrowed and she drew very close.

"I love you like a brother," she said, hugging me with one arm, "and I love you like a mother." Letting go, she proceeded down the hallway, and then yelled over her shoulder, "I'm just doing what mothers do. Ha ha."

Those of us very close to Mother Angelica were practically considered adjunct members of her religious community—spiritual charges, who, whether we requested it or not, were to submit to her occasional counseling and corrections. I remember once privately mentioning some of my confusion about Mother's public lessons in humility to Father Benedict Groeschel. In his wry New Yorkese style he counseled, "Relax . . . humiliation can be the beginning of humility." Didn't I know it. This was apparently the approach that Mother wholeheartedly embraced.

There was one particular moment in our relationship that Mother would occasionally reference in mixed company. "We had words once," she would say. "Raymond didn't get to use any of them."

Among the nuns, she would recall, eyes fixed on yours truly: "We had a little thing once—but it made us love each other more, didn't it?" I have never revealed the details of our "little thing," but this seems the appropriate place to do so.

In 1997, Pope John Paul II had announced a pastoral trip to Cuba. It was to be a landmark historical event. As EWTN's news director, live coverage and commentary on the trip were my responsibility. At the network there were certain individuals (long gone) who wanted to shape our coverage to suit their own political perspective—mainly to establish that Cuban president Fidel Castro was a neutral or even positive actor in the region. This tracked with the views of some in Latin America, markets where EWTN was attempting to secure carriage. My intention was to fairly report on the state of the Cuban people and the Castro government while focusing on the message of religious freedom and human rights that would be at the core of John Paul's public statements. During the many months of preparation, without my knowing it, individuals tried to persuade Mother that I was attempting to "politicize" our coverage with a strongly American bias that would hurt the network's prospects in South and Central America.

A few weeks before the Pope touched down in Havana, at a meeting to coordinate the papal event, with

about twenty people present, including Mother Angelica, the "politicization" charge was raised by two coworkers. Mother was in a testy mood that day. What I
didn't know at the time was that she had been taking
high doses of steroids to quell a life-threatening asthma
episode. She had also been fed a lot of misinformation
about my work and my intentions. In front of everyone,
she tore into me, running through a litany of grievances,
including a critique of my "worldly" interview style.
Doug Keck, the vice president of production, recognizing what was happening, tried to run interference, but
Mother flatly told him to "shut up." Turning back to me
she continued: "You could use a bit of humility. I have a
rule when I deal with the sisters. As St. Benedict said,
'When in doubt, give the community, not the individual, the benefit of the doubt.' We need to all consider
the network first!" After what seemed like a ten-minute
screed she stopped.

"Are we finished?" I asked, folding my arms defiantly.

"I'll let you know when I'm finished," Mother said.
Swiftly, the conversation turned to other matters, and I
marched up to my office with every intention of quitting
that day.

Doug Keck assured me that the moment would blow
over and urged me to keep my head. The injustice of
the empty charges stung, as did the suggestion that I
was somehow not considering the overall good of the
network. The public dressing-down from this woman

whom I respected had also wounded my pride. But I knew how important the live papal coverage was to the network and how much energy and money had already been expended to pull it off. Out of professional courtesy, I elected to anchor the papal visit to Cuba . . . then I would leave.

The first night of the Cuba coverage, on January 21, was a smash. Our commentary was authoritative, and since the Monica Lewinsky/Bill Clinton story had broken earlier that day, we were the only broadcast outlet covering the visit wall to wall. The audience was thrilled by what they saw coming from Cuba. When I got off air and up to my office it was late, maybe 9:30 p.m. The phone rang. It was Mother Angelica.

"That was the most beautiful, professional, uplifting papal event we have ever had on this network. It was awesome. Spiritually powerful and so professional."

Still licking my wounds I had to ask, "Is this an apology?"

There was silence on the line. "You were wonderful. Good night sweetheart." And she hung up the phone.

It may not have been the apology I was seeking, but it was the only apology Mother could offer. For a woman who had been abandoned by the first man in her life, she found it difficult to trust men—particularly men who stood their ground—so apologies came hard. Aside from the passing mentions noted above, we never directly spoke of that event again. But it proved to be a decisive turning point in our relationship. From that time on Mother rarely questioned my judgment, and a new-found trust blossomed between us that would endure to the end of her life.

Mother Angelica tested me at that moment. It was a tactic she would also use in the monastery to prune the faults of her sisters. She scolded me in public and pushed hard to get a reaction. In retrospect, I think she was smoking me out, trying to see what I was really made of. Thankfully, I walked through the fire, respected her throughout, and swallowed my pride—a good thing since she had much more to teach me. Mother never again mentioned my lack of humility in public. What she said in private is for me to know. . . .

Broadcast Lessons

MY VERY FIRST live show appearance on February 21, 1996, in some ways set the standard for all my broadcast encounters with Mother Angelica. On that date I joined Mother and a group of EWTN vice presidents to unveil a series of initiatives, among them the news division. As fate would have it, a nasty case of laryngitis stole my voice that night. Mother found it hilarious that I was reduced to a whisper.

"This is an answer to prayer," she said before the show, "because you're so loud any other time no one else would be heard. Oh, the Lord has a sense of humor, don't He?"

I was glad somebody was laughing.

Among the many things Mother taught me was a sense of ease in front of the camera. I was a bit theatrical when I first came to the network owing to my acting background. As an actor and a "professional" broadcaster I was accustomed to writing out my best lines and rehearsing for any public appearance, particularly on live television. One night when I was cohosting the show with Mother sometime in 2000, she caught me reviewing my notes on set before the broadcast. With thirty seconds till showtime, Mother plopped into the upholstered chair next to mine.

"What you reading?"

"Just some notes. Things I want to say."

She cocked her head to the side. "Can I see?"

I reluctantly handed the notes to her as the show's theme music filled the studio.

She looked down at the papers derisively. "What do you need these for?" she asked, and with that tore the pages in four. Sweat started beading through the pancake on my forehead.

"This is about a brother talking to a sister and a sister talking to a brother," she instructed, waving the ripped paper to underscore her point. "The show happens here between us, not on some paper." Then looking at the camera, she shoved the shredded notes under the edge of her chair cushion and started the show. "Hello family, well we've got Raymond with us tonight."

At this point, I was a sweaty mess without a life preserver, my best lines now turned to confetti. Still, the show ended up being a fun, rollicking ride, which was often the case owing to our natural chemistry and affection. Of course, Mother was right. Rehearsals are needed, but there is a point where you have to leave all of it behind and just connect with your partner in front of the camera. She also gave me permission to have a good time and to allow my humor to come to the surface. No one understood the power of humor like Mother. It was the secret to her success on television and partially explained her hold on millions.

Over the years people have complimented me on this interview or that. What many of them don't realize is that it was Mother Angelica who taught me how to let go and have a real conversation with my guests. She was a natural, one who didn't carry the weight of self-awareness that so many of us lug around in television. Mother hadn't even seen a television show until the 1960s and had little time to watch afterward. Her broadcast lesson to me was simple and wise: be who you are, and if you truly share yourself with the person sitting opposite you, memorable, unexpected things will happen. In a way it was yet another Angelica master class in humility. I guess I didn't know everything about TV or performing after all.

Living in the Present Moment

IT TOOK ME five years to complete Mother's biography. Thanks to our "little thing," she offered me some of the most candid interviews of her life over a three-year period starting in 1999. I was stunned by the frankness of those interviews and the way she willingly shared so many personal details never before disclosed. It took me a year to write the manuscript, and Doubleday set the release date for September 6, 2005.

For my family, it was an exciting time. We were expecting our third child, Mariella, at the end of August, the biography was coming out, and a three-month book tour awaited. Everything was moving along just as planned.

Then on August 16, we rushed my wife to Mercy Medical Center in New Orleans, earlier than expected, for the birth of our baby. Though we were thrown by the early arrival, little Mariella was healthy, and so was Mama. I resumed my weekly trips to Birmingham to shoot the live show, and plans were quickly back on track.

In Birmingham, during the wee hours of Saturday, August 27, I could not sleep. I flipped on the TV and watched the landfall projections for a massive, Category 5 hurricane swirling in the Gulf: Katrina. At the time it was to make landfall somewhere east of New Orleans, most likely in the Florida Panhandle, according to the

National Weather Service. There was great confusion in the Big Easy about whether to evacuate the city or ride out the storm.

Over time New Orleanians have acquired a rather blasé attitude about these storms. Usually a prayer to Our Lady of Prompt Succor and a Sazerac are enough to avoid an evacuation, or at least enough to put your mind at ease until the National Guard comes to remove you from the house. But when I saw the tracking maps and considered the hateful power of this hurricane, I knew we could take no chances. With an infant under the roof it was too risky. I called Rebecca immediately and told her to pack up the children and the necessary things. Once I landed in New Orleans later that morning, we would evacuate for a few days—just to be on the safe side.

For many years, Mother Angelica had counseled me to "live in the present moment." I have to admit that I found the concept confusing. Whenever she saw me running between events at the network or fretting over some looming project, she would always say, "You better learn to live in the present moment. It's the only way you'll ever get anything done."

One afternoon in her office when we had some time alone, I asked her to elaborate. She said, "I have never had a problem focusing. Never have. See, I live in the present moment. One of the saints said, 'The past is dead. The future unknown. The present moment is all we have.' You see when I'm here at the network, I forget about where I just was and I'm not focusing on what's next. I'm just *here*."

Later, under my relentless questioning, she would make this practical spirituality even more explicit. "We have to learn to live in the present moment. We have to ask God: What are you calling me to do now, in this present moment? Not yesterday, not tomorrow, but *right now*. God's will is manifested to us in the duties and experiences of the present moment. We have only to accept them and try to be like Jesus in them."

Like a child who hears a parent repeat a phrase so often that he begins to tune it out, I must confess, Mother's "present moment" advice was duly noted but certainly not an organic part of my life. That was, until Katrina struck.

The eight-hour journey from New Orleans up to Hanceville, Alabama, was arduous, especially for Rebecca and the baby. We had packed four days' worth of clothes, a few pictures, some videos, my Sinatra CDs, the two boys, and my mother-in-law into the van and fled town. Mother Angelica and her vicar, Sister Catherine, graciously allowed us to stay at their guest house until the storm passed. Again, Reverend Mother was there, doing what mothers do—watching after her loved ones.

Once Katrina blew by the city, we thought we were out of the woods, but the drainage pumps were never engaged in our area. The house took on seven feet of water, destroying most of our possessions. Leather coats were turned to slime in our closets, the dining room table had flattened into a shapeless brown sponge, and black mold decorated every wall of the house. It is a wrenching feeling to know that you have lost not only your belongings and so many memories, but also the geography of your past. The places where you grew up, where you ate Sunday dinners, where you bought your first record are all gone. Gone. It is hell wanting to go home, knowing full well that home is no longer there. We really just wanted to stay in our beds at the nun's guest house and not get up. That's when I embraced the present moment.

Mother's speech was greatly diminished by 2005. During my visits at the monastery she would stroke my face and assure me that "It'll be okay." She prayed with me and the family, and though she couldn't pronounce them at the time, the memory of her words were burned into my mind: *God's will is manifested to us in the duties and experiences of the present moment. We have only to accept them and try to be like Jesus in them.* In days I was supposed to begin a media tour months in the making for a book that I had devoted five years of my life to producing. Given the circumstances, I considered canceling the tour and staying in Birmingham with my family. Our son was in a new school; the house in New Orleans needed tending to. Still, Rebecca and I decided that I should go on the tour as planned.

Homeless and not sure of our next step, all we had to cling to were the prayers of the nuns and the lodgings they offered us. It was one of those moments when you throw yourself into God's hands and pray that he will guide you.

I sought comfort in the onerous tour schedule and the relentless travel. I remember being in New York for the major media swing of the tour. This was to be the book's big coming-out party. I was booked on a string of major cable and network shows. When I rose early to make my morning TV hits, I noticed that my hotel was filled with Secret Service agents. Turns out the president was at the UN; Michael Brown, the FEMA director, had just resigned; and John Roberts's Supreme Court confirmation hearings were under way in the Senate. Needless to say, morning to night, I got bumped off of every show where I had been scheduled to appear. When news is breaking, guests talking about their books are the first to go. To say that I was depressed about this horrible turn of events would be an understatement. To distract myself, I walked to the theater district and bought a ticket to a play about a nun that I had heard good things about. It was appropriately called *Doubt*.

As I dashed to the theater to make the curtain, my cell phone rang. It was my editor at Doubleday informing me that the Mother Angelica biography had hit the *New York Times* bestseller list.

We have to ask God: What are you calling me to do

*now, in this present moment? Not yesterday, not tomor-
row, but right now.*

At that moment, He was calling me to celebrate! Which I did. I paid a guy to snap a cheesy picture of the *New York Times* best-selling author in Times Square. It is a reminder that no matter how dark a situation may be or how confusing, God is there in each present moment if you keep moving forward and trusting.

On reflection, though hundreds of thousands of people were negatively affected by Hurricane Katrina, in time it became one of the great blessings of our lives. We would never have resettled in Virginia had it not been for Katrina, never met so many dear friends, and never had the opportunity to live on pure faith. And I don't see how I would have survived any of it or known its richness without Mother and her insistence that I live in the present moment. It has since become one of the great guiding principles of my life. Lesson learned, Mama.

Fearlessness and Freedom

SEVERAL HOURS SPENT in daily prayer furnished Angelica with a keen ear for God's call, a call she would instantly act upon. Her sense of purpose, her dedication in the aftermath of one of these divine calls was something to behold. Once Mother felt compelled by God to accomplish some end, there was no stopping her.

How many of us would dare to begin a cable television network in a suburban garage with literally no experience at the age of fifty-eight? Now imagine that you were physically disabled, broke, and a cloistered nun. Few would believe that such a scenario could work out. Unless you knew Mother Angelica.

I remember her return from a trip to Bogotá, Colombia, in 1996. Mother was convinced that the Child Jesus had appeared and instructed her to build Him "a temple." Once she figured out that a temple could be a church, she was off to the races. Having already begun building a monastery in Hanceville, she quickly adapted her plans to suit the message received. Soon she and the sisters were picking out rare marbles and ordering custom stained glass to fulfill what Mother considered a "questionable" command. No matter the doubts, she did as she was told. There were those at the time who quibbled about the expense and the grand scale of the shrine rising in Hanceville. Some even doubted it would ever be completed. Undaunted by the criticism, Mother, on television, accused the naysayers of desiring "the very least for God, but only the best for [themselves]."

Her faith protected her, suppressing the trepidation and fear that often stop new initiatives. During one of our interviews, I asked Mother if she had any personal fears when she started the network. She replied, "You have to know a lot about something to be scared, and I didn't know anything, so I didn't know what to be scared about."

I like to think that some of her fearlessness rubbed off on me. Every time I take on a new challenge or a project I've never attempted before, I always think of Mother. She told me once: "We must be unafraid of ridicule or human respect, unafraid to walk out alone, knowing that we are nothing and can do nothing on our own. But with His grace and His power you can do all things." Her life was a living monument to that faithful approach. In the end, it wasn't about Mother, but about whether God permitted something to happen or not.

There was a method she used to deal with inspirations that I have tried to emulate in my own life. Mother would honor each inspiration, praying about it at length. Then she would get to work, valiantly attempting to make the inspiration a reality. She had that delightfully mad Franciscan knack of rushing in where even the fallen angels feared to tread. She described it this way:

"Once I feel something is from God, I start out with a sincere heart and mind. Even if I have a doubt about something, I just keep at it. Then God begins to show Himself." In the end, God would either open a door and allow her to succeed or stop her efforts cold, clearly indicating that Mother's will was operating and not the Almighty's. It proved a liberating way to work and made her entirely reliant on God's Providence—the source of her confidence and success.

Mother would work like a dervish to finish a project or fulfill a call, even to the point of illness. But she was utterly detached from the aftereffects of those projects.

The results were up to God alone. She had completed her part of the deal. "I'm free in spirit," she would proudly declare. "I'm free in my heart because what I do, I do for God." There were no ulterior motives in Mother's work. So many people can be self-serving, doing things for glory, power, or the affections of others. Not Mother. "If you like me or you don't, I don't care. . . . I don't give a damn," she confided to me privately. Her Spouse was the only audience she really cared about.

This disregard for human accolades allowed her to stand by her principles, serve God without division, and speak uncomfortable truths when needed, even when it was not in her personal interest to do so.

"If you're not a thorn in somebody's side, you're not doing Christianity right," she would say from time to time. And Angelica did Christianity right.

I'll never forget leaving to cover my first Bishops' Conference meeting for EWTN in the late 1990s. As I prepared to make my way to the airport, I bumped into Mother Angelica in a network hallway. When I informed her that I was en route to D.C. for the bishops' meetings, she placed a hand on my shoulder and with a slight smirk counseled: "Remember, it is better to have their fear than their love." Having clashed with a few hostile bishops over everything from inclusive language in the liturgy to the right to broadcast, Mother spoke from her own painful experience. "You should try to love them, but don't expect much in return," she said.

One of the smartest priests in the Church, in my presence, once tried to sell Mother on the notion of a for-profit national Catholic radio operation. "It won't work. It has to be nonprofit," Angelica declared definitively.

"Look, Mother, Franciscans do things one way and we do things another," the priest said.

"It won't work."

"Well, pray for us, Mother."

"You don't need my prayers. You need St. Jude's prayers," she shot back, invoking the patron saint of impossible causes. Mother felt obligated to speak the truth even at the risk of upsetting friends. The for-profit radio venture lasted eighteen months before going out of business, losing millions of dollars.

On another occasion a wealthy Catholic wrote Mother a large check to air a series of prayers on her network. She happily accepted the check and ordered the commercial-like spots to be created. Once the prayers began airing, the donor called demanding that they be shown at certain hours to his specifications. She returned his money that day and continued airing the spots where she felt they would reach the audience most in need. Mother was not for sale; neither was her television schedule. As of this writing the prayers are still airing, randomly, on EWTN.

Mother's freedom and fearlessness came from the same place. They were rooted in her vibrant faith—a faith ever receptive to the commands of God and closed to the concerns of man and mammon.

Forgiveness and Sacrificial Love

THROUGHOUT HER LONG career in the public eye, Mother was assailed by clerics, lawyers, nuns, and business tycoons. At various points she was derided as an "archconservative," a "witch," or a "schismatic." She moved so fast that most of the assaults bounced right off the hull of the USS *Angelica*. But on certain occasions, I could see the toll of the salvos in her red-rimmed eyes or in her general sense of weariness. When one is attacked from the outside it is easier to absorb than when the blows come from within—particularly when they originate in the Church. It is all the more painful when the charges are untrue. Mother knew what that felt like.

I remember spending long afternoons with her in 2000 discussing the totally fabricated charge that she had taken money from EWTN to finance the construction of her monastery. After all she had sacrificed for the Church, the accusations hurt. Mother was justifiably angry with those who had leveled the fictitious charges and instigated a Vatican investigation, which, at the time, she was subject to. She recounted several other accusations, and then our conversation took a spiritual turn.

"I've already forgiven them and thanked God for the

trial. We have to forgive instantly. That's what the Lord did," she told me. "The actions of your enemy are nothing compared to what you are doing to yourself because of his actions. Your memory is so filled with anger and hurt feelings that it cannot hold anything good. But if you show mercy and forgiveness toward your enemies, you can blamelessly live in the present, and God will take care of the rest."

I did not realize when I heard Mother speak those words how important they would become later, when I faced my own trials.

This is not the place to reopen old scars or to resurrect unjust situations long past. Suffice it to say that I was repeatedly subjected to things we all go through sooner or later. People you thought were friends suddenly turn, whether through jealousy or just plain weakness, and attempt to destroy your work or you personally. They employ familiar tactics: calumnies, distortions, and outright lies. It's a reminder of the powerful sway sin can exert over souls. And when you are doing good work it will inevitably attract that which is not good. As Goethe writes in one of my favorite lines: "There is strong shadow where there is much light."

In my case, at least I had witnessed Mother deal with similar situations and was internally prepared to react. That doesn't mean that I did everything right or that it didn't hurt like hell. It did. The knowledge that the charges were false and the relentlessness of the attacks were demoralizing. I remember sharing similar thoughts with a nun very close to Mother. She smiled sweetly and said, "If you had done something wrong, it wouldn't be a persecution. . . . Get into the habit of thanking God for every persecution—so you don't become like the people doing this to you." Her words allowed me to defend myself, while not permitting the anger over the situation to consume me. In fact, I did some of my best work during those periods, all the while attempting to summon as much mercy as I could muster.

If you show mercy and forgiveness toward your enemies, you can blamelessly live in the present, and God will take care of the rest.

He really does take care of the rest. Sudden unforeseen turns of events, illnesses, or unexpected individuals intrude, resulting in some type of justice. Sometimes you get to see it, and sometimes not. But the Almighty's resolution is always infinitely more interesting than anything you can devise. The point is to forgive quickly and allow God the space to work in you and in your enemy. We may also need that same forgiveness and mercy someday.

OF ALL THE CHAPTERS in this book, this one has been the most difficult to write. Reporting is much easier than describing the intimate ways another life has altered your own. For a son, describing what he learned from his spiritual mother is ultimately an impossible task. It is not her words, in the end, but her example that I hold closest to my heart.

I remember one night at EWTN, many years ago, busloads of people had come to see Mother's live show. I was cohosting that evening. She was very ill at the time, battling asthma, and in the midst of a conflict with Cardinal Roger Mahony over a passing comment she had made on her program a few weeks earlier. She had been in meetings at the network all day, hosted her live show, and was now taking individual pictures with hundreds of people in studio. When Mother finished, she looked as if she had been thrown down a couple of staircases.

Outside a car was waiting to take her on the long trip back to the monastery. I offered to walk her out. As I opened the car door, I spied two busloads of fans in the distance, rounding the turn. "Get in the car, Mother, before they see you," I told her. But it was too late. The first bus screeched to a halt on the other side of Mother's vehicle. Retired groupies began beating on the windows and waving as the lights came on. Then the door of the bus opened.

"Go ahead. I'll tell them how tired you are," I said.

Mother shut the car door and stepped back. "They're old and tired. They've come a long way," she croaked.

"You're old and tired and you have a long way to *go*. Why don't you get in the car?"

But she was having none of it. Mother shook her head

with a smile, made her way to the front of the vehicle, sat on the hood, and signed autographs. She remained there, coughing in the night air, for at least forty-five minutes—chatting, hugging, and, I knew, suffering for her family. It was a great display of the love she had for her audience, an example of generosity and humility that everyone in public life should model. I still see her now on the hood of that car, thronged by so many over-joyed people. How different that image would be from my last meeting with Mother—and how similar.

CHAPTER 6

Drowsing to Glory

My soul is longing and pining for the courts of the Lord; my heart and my flesh sing for joy to the Living God.

—PSALM 84:2

SHE IS RARELY AWAKE. The carnation-pink skin practically glows. Her head lies to one side on an immaculate white pillow. She heaves heavily, snorting every so often—dozing her way into eternity. When she does awaken it is as if she has suddenly returned from a foreign land. She seems disoriented at first, as if this room and the faces surrounding her are unknown. Mother Angelica is now a stranger in the place where she has spent fifteen years of her life. She is nearer another home.

"Mother! Mother! Raymond is here!!!" the diminutive Sister Gabriel is yelling into her ear as if she were a football field away. "Come on, Mother!! Mother!!"

The old nun's eyelids flutter. She fights back the sleep that occupies so much of her day. When she comes to, reentering the room, she sees me. There is a flicker of recognition, a familiar weak smile. She nods her head and offers the heavily veined hand I know so well. The high jinks and the jokes are gone. Even the rolling eyes and exasperated expulsions of air that were once her main means of communication have left her. She valiantly tries to focus on my greeting, to hear the news from the outside world, but sleep—the pull of what is on the other side—snatches her fiercely away. The eyelids droop and she is gone once more, though not completely. As she slumbers, Mother Angelica's hand is like a vise. It holds fast to those of us on this side of life. The hand pulses firmly, never losing its grip.

She is moving these days. There is an ethereal serenity about the whole scene. Sisters Gabriel, Regina, Emmanuel, and Michael float in and out of the room, one of them always maintaining their vigil. Mother sleeps for hours and hours each day. The room is quiet now, exactly as she likes it.

"She's very obedient to the Lord's will," Sister Gabriel tells me as she looks down at the woman for whom she has cared for so long. "Whatever the Lord asks of her, she does it. Even this: more than a decade of suffering in bed, this heavy cross. And she's happy and content. She taught me how to accept the cross and suffer. Sometimes she still complains, but that's human nature. This is a time for me to help Mother, when she needs me. It's a way for me to repay her for the gift she has given me."

There is sadness in Gabriel's voice. She pauses, looking down at Reverend Mother, and then quickly turns and slides a rolling table into the corner to stem the emotion rising to the surface. No time to think about the future. There is much to do in the present moment: oxygen levels to balance, medicines to be laid out, meals to be prepared, socks to be folded, sponge baths, and nail clipping, and hair brushing—so much to be done.

The care these sisters provide has permitted Mother Angelica to stay as long as she has—and she has not wasted a moment of the time.

Watching her rest in bed, her thin body shifting beneath the flannel sheets, I recall something she told me long ago: "One of the lessons I've learned is that suffering and old age are most precious. You know why? Because at that point in our lives, we're powerful."

Mother meant that the elderly and infirm enjoy long hours with God alone, hours to pray and intercede for others. It is a mysterious power, but it is a power nonetheless. Just as their bodies weaken, their spirits are emboldened. As death draws near, fears diminish. So does interest in the material world.

These last years of spiritual and physical pruning—"old age"—had transformed Mother Angelica. She was totally detached from the things of this life. Radiant and serene, she is ready to see God face to face.

During one of my visits with her in 2008, I received a
profound glimpse into Mother's intensely personal experience. For the better part of a half hour she opened her
mouth, licking her lips as if she wanted to say something.
Each time the effort resolved into a low "Hmmm." Then
she squeezed my hand and very slowly, as if she didn't
want to disturb what was to come, she pronounced with
great care: "At . . . the . . . end. He takes . . . every . . .
everything. Away." She smiled once it was out—a wearied smile of accomplishment and acceptance. So many
things had been taken from Mother in those last years:
her mobility, her voice, her authority, her freedom—but
not her faith and certainly not her powers of intercession.

Power and Glory

MAKING SENSE OF her years of silence—years away
from the public just when people needed her most—is
a chore. Mother's stroke hit at the end of 2001, shortly
before the clergy sex abuse crisis commanded headlines
in Boston and became a nationwide scandal. In time, the
ugly horror would strike the Church in other countries,
outside the United States. In the ensuing years there
would be Vatican Bank exposés, leaked correspondence
to and from the Holy Father, court battles over religious
liberty, an unexpected papal retirement, and the enig-
matic reign of Pope Francis. Through it all, Mother remained in her room at the monastery, in union with God.

I turned to her sisters to put this period of silence, Mother's extended retreat from the public, in context and to opine on her lengthy confinement.

"I know that she built the network in part for those who were housebound and she is now one of them," Sister Grace Marie told me while Mother was restricted to her cell. "I would imagine that she is praying for the church and for the Holy Father. . . . Who is to say that the suffering that Mother has endured isn't more efficacious than all she did before? She's totally abandoned—and that constant 'yes' to God's will, in her suffering, is such a witness to me. But that's the economy of God; He takes what the world considers useless and makes it valuable. He comes not to take suffering away, but to sanctify it. And she is still teaching us, even in this, how to suffer well. . . . From being such a communicator to someone who cannot communicate. That acceptance of God's will is huge. . . . Given all she has put up with, she's a saintly woman. She's such a lesson for me."

"As soon as Mother had her stroke, I prayed that His Will be done. To do otherwise would be like asking Jesus to come down off the cross—as if you can't do any good up there," Mother Dolores Marie explained. "This is the suffering that [the Lord] asked her to do now. She is suffering for all of us, for the Church, and to get her own soul ready for heaven. It is very fruitful. This is her gift to us. As John Paul said at the end of his earthly life: The elderly are being formed for eternity. This suffering also allowed her to fulfill the love of her vocation: to be a contemplative. Mother is a means to an end, not the end. And so many people got stuck there. God is the end. Mother understood that."

"Her mission is to suffer. She is doing more for the Church and the world now than she did even at EWTN," Sister Catherine (now Mother Gabrielle Marie) said. "Mother is on the cross. She has always suffered so well, never giving in to the pain she had to endure or the illness. That was a great grace God gave her. To be in bed all these years in such pain, and with such resignation— she's a living saint."

Sister Consolata, who spent many years in Mother's cell caring for her, summed up the protracted retreat this way: "I think that Reverend Mother had permission to speak for a number of years and her mission now is to only speak to God. The years of dead silence have been a gift from her to the Lord; a chance to converse with the Lord very intimately. She gave lessons about this—that when you are elderly your mission becomes solitary with the Lord. Part of it is her penance. . . . Silence in the heart is union with God, and that is always healing. The graces of her suffering are definitely for the community and for the Church. And the silence is also purifying her. Our strongest virtue can also be our strongest fault. It is a dramatic time of reparation and of penance. She told us at the time of her stroke that she 'wasn't ready.' If this is not the mission of suffering that she preached, I don't know what is. The Lord is using her to witness to the value of suffering, infirmity, and even being an invalid."

One of the younger nuns who left the monastery offered this appraisal: "Personally, I think God has chosen her to be a victim soul. Her silence and suffering I think are for the community. God has a plan for everything. He doesn't allow something to happen for no reason. I was in the hospital with Mother the day after her brain surgery—she's still my spiritual mother—and it was hard to see her suffering and it is still hard to see her suffering. But God is permitting that. I think Mother is silently suffering for our souls—for the souls of her sisters. This is something that she would have had to give God permission to do. And I would think that God would have asked her to suffer this silence for the community. We were destroying ourselves."

"Those quiet years were to pray for souls, for the world, for our community, for the network," Sister Antoinette believes. "She did so much to prepare for the great chastisement that was to take place; the monastery had its own water supply, electricity, food. It was ready for any kind of external emergency. But it ended up being this internal emergency—a chastisement of the community. And Mother took her daughters through that too."

At times it was a heart-wrenching journey. By 2015, several of the sisters had either returned to secular life or transferred to other religious houses. Through the labors of the remaining sisters and the unceasing spiritual hardships of Mother, healing gradually came to Our Lady of the Angels Monastery. Under the guidance of the visiting superiors, the nuns rediscovered their charism. Following all the changes, Sister Regina, a veteran of more than fifty years at Our Lady of Angels confidently told me, "The roots are still here and from that we can grow."

On September 15, 2015, things came full circle. On that day a Vatican representative read a mandate to the sisters of Our Lady of the Angels. There would be no elections for a new abbess. The Holy See had decided to "merge" St. Joseph's Monastery in Charlotte with Our Lady of the Angels and appoint Mother Dolores Marie the superior of both communities. After initially struggling with the decision to return to Hanceville, Dolores Marie accepted Rome's decision as the will of God. A lesson Mother Angelica imparted to her as a junior helped her to accept the request of the Holy See.

"As I was considering it, I thought about something Mother once said, 'A long time ago I made a promise to our Lord never to deny him anything he asked of me.' It struck me to the heart the moment she said it. And I asked for the same grace," Mother Dolores told me. "Returning to Hanceville was a huge sacrifice because we were so committed to building the monastery in Charlotte . . . but there was an underlying peace that all of the sisters experienced. That was God's grace."

One of Mother Angelica's own daughters would return to lead her community. Five sisters from Charlotte joined Mother Dolores in the motherhouse to continue the restoration. Perhaps this was what Angelica had been waiting for.

Many benefited from the mental and physical sufferings Mother Angelica had endured. Though the public and the sisters felt the reverberations of grace from her adversity, perhaps none felt them more acutely than Mother herself. In a particular way this last trial was personal. Some of her nuns believe that Angelica "spent her purgatory" in that room and readied her soul for heaven there. Others saw reflections of her devotion to the Child Jesus in her final struggles. She assumed the helplessness of the Divine Child and like Him was totally reliant on others for survival.

A line Mother liked to quote, from a letter St. Francis wrote to his community around 1225, captures her last quiet years and could sum up her entire religious life: "Humble yourselves that you may be exalted by Him! Hold back nothing of yourselves for yourselves, that He Who gives Himself totally to you may receive you totally!"

Mother held nothing back, and the fruits of her oblation showed themselves in a special way on the weekend of May 20, 2012.

To commemorate the fiftieth Anniversary of Our Lady of the Angels Monastery, Bishop Robert Baker celebrated a special Mass broadcast on EWTN on May 19. It was more like a reunion than an anniversary. For those familiar with the monastery's history, it felt like an extended curtain call with the lead players coming forward to take one last bow in unison.

Many of the sisters from the satellite monasteries returned to their motherhouse for the special occasion. Standing in the familiar stalls of the Mass choir, behind the high brass grille, were Sister Marie Andre from Arizona, Sister Grace Marie from San Antonio, and even Sister Antoinette from France, stroking her violin.

The male religious community founded by Mother, the Franciscan Missionaries of the Eternal Word—which had just celebrated the twenty-fifth anniversary of its founding—crowded the altar. Old friends, some of whom helped Mother to build the monastery and the network, EWTN executives, even one of Mother's cousins was in attendance. Bishop David Foley who had famously crossed swords with Mother Angelica when he outlawed a traditional style of worship (later formally encouraged and universalized by Pope Benedict) concelebrated the liturgy. Bill Steltemeier, the honorary EWTN chairman, just days before his eighty-third birthday, willed himself into a wheelchair to make an appearance. Sitting at the edge of the congregation, a scarf about his throat, Steltemeier looked ashen and frail. In March of that year, he had been diagnosed with an aggressive form of cancer that would claim his life on February 15, 2013. But he made it his business to be at the celebratory Mass that day, no matter the obstacles.

Mother Angelica was noticeably absent from the anniversary festivities. And though she dozed comfortably in her cell during the Mass, Mother did manage to watch a rebroadcast of the celebration later in the day. She was not able to remain awake throughout. Still she enjoyed what she saw, and must have loved what she heard.

Father Joseph Mary Wolfe, the first man to enter Mother's order of friars, preached at both the Mass and a Vespers ceremony commemorating the fiftieth anniversary of the monastery's founding. In his second homily, Father Wolfe underscored the importance of Mother's witness, declaring, "Can anyone deny that God has revealed in a remarkable way His Divine Providence—that prayer really does move mountains?" Since the anniversary fell on the World Day of Communications, Wolfe quoted from the pope's message on communications, highlighting the connection between the proclamation of the Word and the power of silence. The message might well have been a concise overview of Mother Angelica's last eleven years:

> It is often in silence, for example, that we observe the most authentic communication taking place between people who are in love: gestures, facial expressions and body language are signs by which they reveal themselves to each other. Joy, anxiety, and suffering can all be communicated in silence—indeed it provides them with a particularly powerful mode of expression. . . .
>
> [We] must make space for silent contemplation. Out of such contemplation springs forth, with

all its inner power, the urgent sense of mission, the compelling obligation "to communicate that which we have seen and heard" so that all may be in communion with God.

. . . In silent contemplation, then, the Eternal Word, through whom the world was created, becomes ever more powerfully present and we become aware of the plan of salvation that God is accomplishing throughout our history by word and deed.

With every passing day the Eternal Word had become Mother Angelica's all, and His presence grew more palpable in her cell and far beyond its confines.

Her Heroic Virtues

STRANGERS AND INTIMATES have suggested to me over the years that Mother Angelica is a saint. Since I am neither a member of the Congregation for the Cause of Saints nor an investigator assigned to Mother's cause, I will not presume to leap ahead of the Church and begin printing St. Angelica of Hanceville prayer cards. The truth is, I have been too close to Mother for too long a period to offer a dispassionate judgment. Ultimately, the formal designation of sanctity is best left to the Church. There is a venerable and thorough process for any candidate that should be respected.

That said, the final mark of a saint is not perfection, but lived virtue. It is the striving for holiness through-out the arc of a life that makes a saint. And so while I will not discuss or argue "sainthood" for Mother, I see no harm in exploring a few of the virtues she lived and exemplified to the extreme.

Faith

MOTHER FAMOUSLY SAID, "Faith is one foot on the ground, one foot in the air and a queasy feeling in the stomach." She knew that feeling all too well. From de-serting her mother, Mae, to join a Cleveland monastery at the age of twenty-one, to building a television net-work with no funds in the woods of Alabama, Mother Angelica took mad risks for God. Talking about faith is easy, but Mother acted on it in such a way that the fruits of her efforts became manifest to all. Hers was a gutsy faith.

St. Paul writes in First Corinthians 1:27: "The fool-ish things of the world hath God chosen, that he may confound the wise; and the weak things of the world hath God chosen, that he may confound the strong." By external appearances, Rita Rizzo certainly qualified as both "foolish" and "weak." She had no silver spoon in her mouth, no letters after her name (save for those of her religious order), none of the "right people" swam in her social circle, and she contended with disability and infirmity from her youth. The one thing she did have, once she found God, was a rock-solid faith and a determination never to fail Him.

Despite what people saw on television, Mother's path was littered with fear, spiritual dryness, and occasional darkness. She shared a revealing anecdote with me about the depth of her faith and the strength it lent her during the ordeal of a spinal operation. Just before the surgery the doctor had informed Sister Angelica that she might never walk again. "I was scared. I shook in that bed and was petrified, but I said, 'Lord, I know You'll take care of me.' And believe me, I shook all the way to the operating room," she remembered. "The Lord did take care of me, but not before I had to go through a real purification period. I had to believe when I saw nothing—and seeing nothing is scary. So don't feel bad if you have a similar reaction—if you feel afraid and you question. Don't think for a minute it is because you lack faith. Sometimes all that fear is the road to faith."

She would stare down "that fear" and see "nothing" many times in her life, moving forward in the belief that she was doing God's will. There was no certainty that Angelica could sustain a contemplative religious order in the Protestant Deep South in the early 1960s. Even after all the begging, scraping, and salesmanship, there was no assurance that the public would rally around a start-up Catholic cable network originating from Birmingham, Alabama. Since she had neither theological training nor media experience, there was certainly no assurance that she could craft programming that would attract an international audience. Risking millions of dollars at every turn and constantly raising the stakes, Mother Angelica defied the nothingness before her and leapt into the abyss, relying entirely on God to catch her.

But perhaps at no point in her life did she show more faith or abandon herself to the darkness more readily than during the extended last chapter of her life. Those years were a time of "real purification." She stayed true to God's will, even when she could no longer fully understand His plans. Through it all, she never lost the external piety that had always characterized her faith.

Mother Angelica's love of God was never a private affair or an intellectual exercise, but a lifelong activity to be practiced in public. A friend of Mother's, Steven Zaleski, shared a story from 1943. At that time, Rita Rizzo worked at the Timken Roller Bearing Company. On the corner of her desk was a picture of Jesus wearing a crown of thorns. A coworker accused her of "pushing her religion" in the workplace. Rita turned on the Italian charm, saying, "If you have a picture of a movie star or someone you love, you put it out there. Well this is my Love, and it's going to stay there." She held her Love close, deep into old age, as anyone who saw her excitedly greeting her Spouse in the Blessed Sacrament or gently kissing the bedside statues of Jesus could attest.

In some ways, the entire Shrine of the Most Blessed

Sacrament and the religious images that fill it are enduring monuments to the expressive, tactile faith of Mother Angelica. Nothing was ever too much for her Spouse—not marbled floors or elaborate mosaics or even a diamond-lined tabernacle, His sacramental domicile. But long before she had constructed the Shrine or the Grotto of the Nativity or the elegant Stations of the Cross in Hanceville, her faith had left its mark in Birmingham.

Any visitor to EWTN has seen the rustic, outdoor Way of the Cross near the entrance to the network property. The stations, including a covered Pietà, were built to Mother's specifications, as was a simple shrine made of stained glass and altar furnishings rescued from a shuttered Chicago parish. These "holy reminders" were meant to draw the mind and heart to God throughout the day unceasingly—which is how Mother liked to pray, and live.

Unceasing prayer, she taught, "allows you to turn your entire life into a living prayer . . . Everything you do is for God, though your attention and activity are focused on the duties of your life. This way there is no separation between your life and your prayer; they are woven together like threads in a tapestry."

Faith and action were one in Mother's life. Everything she did was inspired or propelled by her time in prayer. Fulfilling the obligations of her contemplative vocation, she spent set hours each day in the chapel before the

Blessed Sacrament. Even when she didn't feel the joy of His Presence and languished in "dryness," Mother faithfully showed up for her appointed time of adoration as a personal offering. This habit of obedient faith made her receptive to God's will and increased her desire to comply with it. To do so, she exercised that other theological virtue: hope.

Hope

MOTHER ANGELICA HAD a radical belief in and dependence on God's Providence. It was her lived hope that God would be there for her and lead everything to its best ends—even if those ends didn't turn out as she planned. Mother explained it this way:

> God's providence disposes and directs everything for His honor and glory, and for the good of my soul. . . . His providence surrounds me like a cloak. I neither live nor move without it. He keeps the entire universe in order, and still finds time to take a personal interest in you and me.

Mother's deep trust in God's providential care was the source of her hope and confidence. It also explains why she was untroubled by the things she lacked or the actions of others. Her hope in God gave her fortitude.

"The gift of fortitude," Mother taught, "makes us

persevere in holiness. It gives us the strength to forge ahead in the face of opposition and weakness. It gives us supernatural endurance, a spiritual daring." And God knows Mother had that.

The same fortitude that allowed her to embrace pain and physical trials empowered Mother to boldly take an orthodox vision of the Catholic faith into the global marketplace when everyone predicted failure.

Mother zealously marched forward with a determined hope that the Gospel message could change hearts, and that those who were touched would in time support her network. As a monument of her hope and faith, Mother made EWTN entirely reliant on the generosity of its viewers for support. She wanted the network always to be dependent on God's Providence.

EWTN's every move was saturated in prayer and the power of the sisters' perpetual adoration of God. There was a reason Mother put the chapel in Birmingham at the very center of the network complex. This house of prayer was the dynamo that generated the energy for all of EWTN's accomplishments. Mother's hope was that broadcasting God's word would have a powerful effect—whether the programming was seen or not. I can recall her saying once in the 1990s, "Makes no difference if people can see or hear the signal. The fact that the Eternal Word is falling in the street, in homes, in the sands of the desert, and in the jungles is a blessing. The Word will not return void. It has power." Though that thinking caused some indigestion among her coworkers, for Mother it was a perfectly natural rationale for the network's existence. Her singular focus was spiritually reaching souls no matter where they were.

Charity

MOTHER HAD A sincere love and concern for the forgotten, the marginalized, the ignored, the abused—wounded people like her. While the Church spent abundant time and resources on the material well-being of people, Mother attended to the spiritual poverty of the masses. She believed that Americans (and later those in other countries), despite their wealth, were spiritually impoverished. In a letter written in November of 1990 to a Vatican cardinal who had questioned her work, Angelica wrote that she was "evangelizing the poorest of the poor." To her mind, average people needed a spiritual lifeline, and they needed it in their moments of distress and confusion. So she labored to bring faith-inflected guidance and the most potent forces she knew—the Mass, litanies, and the truths of her Faith—into the homes of millions. She created a broadcast empire propelled by constant prayer and sent it out to seven continents, twenty-four hours a day. EWTN remains an enduring sign of Mother's enormous charity toward the confused, the lost, and the struggling.

In her personal life she demonstrated the same concern for others. In 1984, an older couple visiting Our Lady of the Angels Monastery chatted with Mother about the new studio she was constructing at the time. Mother patiently answered their questions but was more concerned about their nourishment. Taking pity on them, she packed sandwiches and bananas into a shoebox so they would have something to eat on the long drive back to Florida. Only later did it become apparent that Mr. and Mrs. Bomberger didn't really need Mother's charity. They were actually quite wealthy and ran a philanthropic foundation. In gratitude for Mother's kindness, the Bombergers would later contribute $150,000 to complete EWTN's studio.

Money meant nothing to Mother Angelica. Though she begged for funds, she had no attachment to money. It was a means to an end, a tool to advance God's will. Whether it was five dollars or five million, Mother treated money as a gift entrusted to her by God. Consequently, it was not uncommon for Angelica to pull a wad of cash from under her habit and generously tip a waiter or assist people she encountered who were in need. A woman once wrote Mother Angelica requesting prayers when she and her son were left without income or furniture by a runaway spouse. Having personal experience with that situation, Mother assured the woman of her prayers and sent along rent money as well as a delivery of new furniture. The recipient of Mother's kindness approached me at a book signing to express her thanks.

Sister St. John, a Poor Clare of Perpetual Adoration,

also shared a story of Mother's charity—and how she doggedly urged the nun to accept her religious vocation. As a laywoman, St. John worked at EWTN and would often bump into Mother Angelica. When the topic of a possible vocation came up, the young woman would attempt to redirect the conversation or offer excuses. One day, after many such talks, St. John told the abbess she couldn't enter the convent because she had "a bill to pay that I can't leave my mother with." Later that day, Angelica called her to the monastery parlor.

"She had all the cash on her," St. John reported.

"What is your excuse now?" Mother Angelica asked. "You have to walk up to the edge of the cliff like this. . . . You have to have the faith to take the step, as scary as it is." Sister St. John has been a member of Mother Angelica's order since 1996.

The full expression of Mother's faith, hope, and charity can be most clearly seen in her fervent evangelization efforts. Angelica could not accept the idea that people should be left in the dark, with no light to guide their paths. She corrected error, articulated the truths of the Catholic faith, and became its greatest pitchwoman. Many have written and spoken of the New Evangelization. Mother Angelica *was* the New Evangelization. She brought to fruition the Scripture verse that inspired her to found the radio operation in 1992: "And I saw another angel flying through the midst of heaven, having the eternal gospel, to preach unto them that sit upon the earth and over every nation and tribe and tongue and people" (Rev. 14:6). Mother brought her joyful, no-nonsense, traditional vision of Catholicism to television, the Internet, shortwave, satellite, and terrestrial radio in multiple languages—and audiences couldn't get enough. She spoke like the people watching and elevated their thoughts and souls while they laughed.

It was her zeal and love for souls that made EWTN possible and kept it going for more than thirty years. Louise F. Massa, a longtime viewer, captured it best when she wrote that Mother Angelica was "the Roy Hobbs of the Catholic Church, the 'Natural' who came out of nowhere, and filled the needs of souls that deeply hungered for God. Programming back in the early days of EWTN was spontaneous, and Mother Angelica was the producer of all that spontaneity, her goal was to talk and teach about Jesus, and that she did without hesitation, allowing nothing to get in her way."

Her constant prayer and striving for sanctity made Mother irresistible on air. Other television personalities have their moment and fade away; they enlighten or entertain, but rarely alter the existence of those watching. Mother Angelica was different. She redirected the lives of her viewers and she will continue to have an impact in the future.

The Lasting Touch

IT IS ALWAYS fascinating to discover just who has seen Mother Angelica, and the unique impression she has left upon them. I'll never forget interviewing the gifted actor Anthony Hopkins in 2011. When he asked where our conversation would air, my answer inevitably led to talk of Mother Angelica.

"Oh, the funny nun! Is she Jesuit?" the non-Catholic Hopkins earnestly asked, his eyes aflame. "Yes, yes, I've seen her, she's quite hilarious. She is really like a psychologist. Her understanding of men and women is amazing. One day she was talking about how if a woman passed a window and saw a dress she liked, no matter what she told her husband, you could rest assured she would return and get that dress—with or without him. Very good she is."

A friend, Becky Cipollone, told me about her little daughter, who asked one afternoon: "What does the Virgin Mary do?" Becky answered simply that "the Virgin Mary helps Jesus." The child looked up and announced, "There is another lady that helps Jesus."

"I said 'who?'" Becky recalled. "She took me upstairs to our nightstand, where the prayer book you edited was lying. 'There's the other lady that helps Jesus,' the child said. And she was pointing at Mother Angelica."

Mother possessed what Pope John Paul II called "the feminine genius," which he described in his encyclical

Redemptoris Mater as "the self-offering totality of love; the strength that is capable of bearing the greatest sorrows; limitless fidelity and tireless devotion to work; the ability to combine penetrating intuition with words of support and encouragement."

Taken all in all, she was a woman—a woman armed with an unerring intuition and a mother's heart. Angelica understood that people needed her wise counsel as well as her example. She offered both, and left a legacy that goes on and on.

This letter from Katie Walker came to me in 2012:

> I was born in 1994, so it always comforts me to know that Mother Angelica has been imbuing the airways with her saintly sagacity before my life even began. Although I'm a cradle Catholic, my family never really discovered Mother Angelica until my early teens. . . .
>
> During those turbulent years of temptation, her warm, grandmotherly manner [conveyed] the awesome potency of Confession and the grandeur of Holy Communion. The way she refers to her Bible rarely failed to banish my anger or anxiety, and her humor in the face of social ills is the sure cure for any adolescent's moodiness.
>
> In addition, my family has battled everything from cancer to autism. . . . Mother's esteem for the sacrifice involved in infirmities large or small, physical or emotional remains close to our hearts.

Sometimes, my nonverbal six-year-old brother's babbling garners surprised looks from passersby and my mother often hearkens back to Mother's wise advice to "embrace the Cross" when one is ostracized.

I cannot describe my boundless regard for this virtuous woman, but, rest assured, if I one day have a family of my own, my children will learn to love Mother Angelica and her network as deeply as I do.

Even small children are not immune to Mother's charms—including Patti Martin's little boy:

I listen to Mother throughout the day. After I had my son I noticed that he would crawl into the room and watch the TV whenever Mother was on. He would watch Mother say the Rosary, re-runs of her talk show . . . any time he heard her voice on the tube. I also noticed that other than Mother, he would never even look at the TV. This continues today and he is now two years old. . . . Watching my son give Mother so much attention drew my eye, and focused my attention on her as well. Mother Angelica has played a huge role in bringing me, for the first time in my life, fully and devotedly into the Church.

Lexie Krakora is another young fan of Mother Angelica's, and an incredibly grateful one:

I am a 13-year-old girl in Westfield, Indiana. . . .
After my grandmother died eight years ago, my
grandfather fell away from the church. My mother
had been away for quite a while and my father was
Methodist. We believed in God but we just didn't
go to church. My grandfather was looking through
the TV channels one day and Mother Angelica
popped up saying, "Remember us between your
gas and electric bills." I guess that little, feisty,
old nun touched his heart, so he watched her
show and she changed my grandfather's life. He
came back to the Church and brought my mother.
My dad became Catholic. I think through my
grandmother's intercession, God, and of course,
Mother Angelica, we came back to the faith.
Thank you, Mother.

Christopher Zaragoza is a millennial who experienced
Mother's touch:

My name is Christopher and I am 14 years old. . . .
I am really blessed of being able to watch Mother
Angelica and her TV Network. She has helped
me a lot in my life. She has brought me closer
to Our Lord and to His Holy Catholic Church.
When ever I feel sad and upset I always listen to
Mother Angelica and she brings the Joy of the
Risen Lord into my life. Many teenagers like to

watch TV shows that are bad like *Family Guy*, *American Dad!*, etc. But I love to watch *Mother Angelica Live* because it makes me a better human being, a better Catholic, student and son. God is my true witness of how much my life has changed because of this poor and simple nun. She has helped me get closer to Our Lord in the Most Blessed Sacrament and that relationship has brought peace and harmony into my life.

The vocations Mother Angelica has inspired and nurtured can never be truly calculated. But the effect of seeing a cheerful, orthodox nun in full habit has radically altered the trajectory of lives like this one:

My name is D. Smith, I am 15-years-old and a sophomore. When I first heard Mother I was flipping through the channels. It was the weekend after my reversion, which took place at our diocesan youth conference. She was telling her vocation story. This shook me up because I had just realized that weekend that the emptiness and echo that was always in my heart was a call to religious life. Hearing her story truly solidified the call for me. That was three years ago. Today I am seriously discerning with the Lafayette Carmelites. A good bit of the thanks must go to Mother!! All the hardships she went through to go where God had called her!! . . . Thank you, Mother Angelica! You have helped so many to answer the call to religious life and priesthood.

This heavily edited letter from Alejandra Sedano was originally more than two thousand words in length:

If it weren't for Mother Angelica founding EWTN, I NEVER would have known Jesus. Although I was born and raised Catholic . . . after my Confirmation at age 15, I left my faith altogether along with most of my family. I became an atheist (I'd be a convenient "agnostic" on good days). I didn't attend Church for 3 years. I was very depressed and struggling with many temptations. I fell into new age practices. I was looking for truth, but I didn't know if God really existed. . . . some time later while Channel surfing, I bumped into Mel Gibson's handsome face. God hooked me through that! It was your *World Over* exclusive interview with him on his movie: *The Passion of the Christ*. At first, when I heard it was a movie on Jesus, I rolled my eyes. After watching for some time, I was intrigued. I had never seen Jesus look so real. . . . I would go back to the same channel to try to see the interview again. I began watching other shows on EWTN. I found out there was so much I didn't know! . . . I went back to Confession and received Jesus in the Most Blessed Sacrament fully aware of whom I was receiving because of what I had learned on EWTN. . . . I fell in love with God and His Church. . . .

If it weren't for Mother Angelica I never would have thought about becoming a nun! Once I started watching EWTN, I would watch this stand-up comedian in a habit. I didn't know they were reruns, but Mother Angelica made me look at nuns in a different way. I didn't know nuns could be fun or that they had a sense of humor! I didn't know what Benediction was, but I watched Mother and the nuns behind the grill adoring Jesus and I was so impressed and awed by their dedication to the Lord. . . .

If it weren't for Mother Angelica founding EWTN, my family (my dad, mom, older sister and baby brother) wouldn't have followed after me in converting back to the faith and returning to the Sacraments. It took years, but one by one, by God's grace all my family came back to the faith! . . .

If it weren't for Mother Angelica, I would have fallen into despair and discouragement. I have had to struggle for 6 years in finding the place where God has called me. . . . Time passed and I read your Biography on Mother Angelica. That scene with Mother complaining to Jesus in the chapel always stuck in my mind. He reminded her that she was His Bride. I was acting just like that. God was purifying me and all I did was resist and complain. . . . Because of Mother's joy in suffering, I could bear my own too. I had a living witness of someone who suffered WITH JESUS, not alone. She said several times that besides her vocation her greatest gift was her suffering because it caused her to rely completely on Jesus. After many years and many sufferings I can say the same. . . . I am now in discernment with a traditional Carmelite Monastery. I ask your prayers for my vocation.

Some people had a false idea of Mother Angelica, until they understood who she really was. Sister Marie Suzanne, OCD, a Discalced Carmelite nun, sent this letter, which demonstrates both the misunderstandings and potency of Mother's example:

Recently I listened to your audio book on the life of Mother Angelica. I have never seen any of her programs and had imbibed some of the prejudice about her from my very liberal Catholic friends. Hearing you speak her words so realistically and understanding what she has done for God has made me ashamed that I held a prejudice against her.

As a cloistered contemplative nun myself, I

admit that her work in beginning a TV network seemed extremely odd to me. I now see it as a very unusual and special mission from God, which has turned out to be an instrument for great good in the lives of millions of people.

Her greatest influence on me personally is the spectacular witness of her trust in Divine Providence. At present my little community is starting a new foundation in northern Vermont. We live in a very poor area and the local people cannot help us much financially. We desperately need a little chapel, choir and a few cells in order to receive more vocations. Our money worries are tiny when compared to the millions Mother trusted God to provide. Yet I spend a huge part of my psychic energy worrying about money. I also have made a vow of poverty and, theoretically, trust Divine Providence to provide everything we really need. So why in practice do I expend all my energy in worry? Well, my trust has been shown up for what it is, pretty poor.

Mother Angelica is right up there with Mother Teresa of Calcutta in living her belief that if you step out to do great things for God, God will provide all the earthly means necessary to accomplish the mission. Now every time my mind starts thrashing over worries, I will remind myself of Mother's accomplishments and try to step out as she did in total trust. Hearing about her story has been a great grace to my own religious life, and I am grateful to you and your very enjoyable talent to portray Mother's own voice. I believe I will live my own religious poverty with much greater peace and trust in the future. After all, we need only $50,000.00, peanuts for God's bank account!

Mother seems to have had a particular influence on men. Some who have watched her for many years experienced personal religious awakenings. One young man, Travis Hatcher, wrote that he is "considering becoming a Franciscan friar" due to Mother Angelica's example and willingness to share her faith. Many priests attribute the first rumbling of their vocations to the abbess, including Father Brad D. Guillory, a priest in the diocese of Lafayette, Louisiana:

> Simply put, I would not be a priest today if it were not for Mother and the guidance I found in her weekly teachings as I was going through my decision to answer God's call in my life. The stroke that took her voice from us happened two weeks before I began seminary formation. I truly miss those words of encouragement she gave us every Tuesday and Wednesday night, especially needed in these troubling times.
>
> Send her my warmest blessings . . . for all she

has done for this parish priest along the Bayou Teche.

From the waterways of southern Louisiana to a terrorist-plagued city in Nigeria, Mother's message found a similar reception wherever it landed. This is a letter from Meshach Chindaba, who describes himself as Mother Angelica's "son in the Faith":

How does a son tell how his mother has touched his life? I am a 14-year-old Catholic and my formation owes so much to EWTN which Mother Angelica established. Apart from my 'Catechist' Bishop Edmund Fitzgibbon of blessed memory, I owe most of my knowledge of the faith to the excellent programmes on this Network. Mother's personal story of her encounter with The Child Jesus on the trip to Bogotá, Columbia, has remained indelible in my memory. Her response to the request of the Divino Niño is an example of total dependence on Divine Providence, and has bolstered my confidence as I collaborate with the Our Lady of Fatima Sisters in Jos Archdiocese to establish a secondary school at Kwal in Kanke Local Government Area.

So my dear Ray, if I were to continue recounting her impact in our lives, your programme will not be sufficient to narrate what Mother has been for me—for she has been just that: Mother! For an African who lives in Jos, Nigeria, whose faith has been sorely tried in the past crisis ridden 11 years, a mother is invaluable. We must thank The Most Holy Trinity and Mater Ecclesia for the gift of this living saint. We shall not ever lose her; for whether here or on in Heaven she will remain Mother. Now talking of the New Evangelization—after John Paul the Great, who has done more than Mother Angelica? Thank you, Mother for Formation! Formation!! Formation!!!

But perhaps the most enduring mark Mother has left on the public is her love of God and her far-reaching devotion to His Word. Nicole Grace Keck captures in this letter what so many feel about Mother:

Even though we do not know one another, I hold you ever dearly in my heart and soul, and prayers. Thank you for making Scripture come alive. You slow it all down and virtually re-enact it so vividly, and with such a great sense of humor and seriousness that the Word becomes a living energy. . . . One of my very favorite shows is the one where you discuss John 21 when our risen Jesus appears on the shores of the Sea of Tiberius, inviting the Apostles to breakfast. When your Heavenly birthday comes, I pray that you and Jesus have a great meal near the seashore in

His full love and friendship, with laughter and in eternal bliss! Thank you for showing me how to live within each word, and for doing it with such passion!

Though she could no longer give voice to God's word, Mother Angelica's passion for it never ebbed. Sister Veronica relayed a story to me about Mother receiving a Bible as a gift. When the sisters presented it to her in her room, "Mother smiled and then growing very serious she looked from the Bible to her wedding ring and back again. For [those in the room] it was a reminder that the word of God can be lived, and a sign of how much Mother respected her vow."

The Healer

"WE'RE HERE, WE LIVE, and when Jesus says, 'come,' our time is over, we see Him face to face," Mother Angelica said near the end of her broadcast career. "I am personally of the opinion that people who have lived their life doing God's will, offering their final sufferings to Him with love in their hearts, go straight to heaven."

If this is the operative divine math, Mother Angelica deserved a first-class direct flight.

She suffered throughout her life, but never more than during those last fifteen years. The loss of speech, the relinquishing of her will and self-mastery, was a supreme sacrifice. Yet even in her confusion, she accepted the in-dignities, the embarrassments, and the weakness of her condition as part of God's plan—His will for her. There were times when the weight of the suffering and the mental anguish ambushed Mother, and her eyes would spill silent tears. Upon witnessing a few of these occa-sions, I heard her soothing words to others come rushing back: "You have to carry on with your life and accept God's will. Does it hurt? Sure it hurts. Is it okay to cry? Sometimes. Jesus cried. Mary cried."

And so did Mother Angelica.

Hers was a life of tribulation and pain offered to God for his mighty purposes. Right up until the end, her suf-fering continued. There were near-constant fevers, infec-tions, and bouts of flu—each of which she miraculously survived. Reviewing the pattern of her journey, pain had often been the precursor to the many graces that moved through Mother Angelica's life. In late August of 2015, just weeks before Rome named Mother Dolores Marie the abbess of the monastery, Mother was choking on her food. It was decided that a feeding tube needed to be in-serted. Mother and the sisters accepted this new burden and the many complications it brought into their daily lives. St. John Chrysostom in his homily on the glory of tribulation said: "Trees that grow in shady and sheltered places . . . become soft and yielding, and they are eas-ily damaged by anything at all; whereas trees that grow on the tops of very high mountains, buffeted by strong

MOTHER ANGELICA   219

winds and constantly exposed to all types of weather, agitated by storms and frequently covered with snow, become stronger than iron."

Mother was —spiritually speaking—stronger than iron, and yet she couldn't stand or feed herself during the last few years of her life. Her final bittersweet act was in some ways a conscious oblation of self. In 2000, following a near-death experience, she shared with me a prayer she had been offering to God: "Lord I want you to use me in any way you want. I don't care what it is. Just don't let me see the fruit."

For the most part she wouldn't see the fruit. But having always considered redemptive suffering a gift, she embraced this last drawn-out trial as she had all those that preceded it. "Whether I am suffering in a physical, mental, or spiritual manner, I resemble Jesus at those moments—and the Father looks at us in our pain and He sees His Son in the most beautiful way. That's what makes you holy. Don't rebel," Mother taught. "Our pain only has meaning when we unite it, out of love, to the suffering of Christ."

From the emotional ailments of her youth—the wounds of abandonment and stomach maladies—to the swollen knees, back difficulties, and asthma of her religious life, pain and suffering were catalysts in Mother's life, and her constant companions. They drove her to undertake new activities and lent her the spiritual strength to bring them to completion. Without her physical suffering she may never have left the Cleveland convent, never have made a deal with God to build a monastery to His glory in the South, never have reached millions and millions of people around the globe through silence.

Mother lived and understood the healing power of suffering. She told me once:

> I realized one day that those who continue to suffer may not be healed, because they are healers themselves.
>
> The greatest gift God has given me since my vocation is pain because I am a proud individual, and with the apostolate God has given us and the work to do, I need to be totally reliant on Him. . . . I have spiritually healed precisely because I have not been physically healed. Suffering is healing. There are those who think the path to holiness is to be healed of bodily suffering, but oftentimes God uses that suffering to change us and to heal our souls.

The last time I saw Mother Angelica was like so many of those final visits. For a long while I held her hand, sharing messages people asked me to pass along and chattering on about my children and work. At times it appeared as if Mother was sinking in a murky pond. She would occasionally rise to the surface, open her rhumy eyes, and then suddenly slip back into the deep. She battled against sleep, blinking and adjusting her body to stay attentive.

Then came the moment when I ran out of things to say and avoided expressing the things I should have. I could feel the finality of that moment and didn't want it to pass. I was so grateful to have known her, and to have been so close to her for so long. I caressed her hand and wept. It was the only way I could say good-bye. Mother released her grip, her mouth gaping open: "Ah . . . ah . . . ah." Tears streamed from her eyes and mine.

"I love you and thank you," I managed to say.

Taking my hand once more she communicated in the only language she still possessed: sighs, squeezes of the hand, and labored blinking.

Sleep would overtake her, but after a few moments she was back again, struggling to focus on my face. She clutched my hand tightly once again, forcing herself to stay when she knew it was time to go. Suddenly I felt like one of those people crowding around her on the hood of that car so many years ago outside the network. I didn't want her to leave, and so she remained as long as she could—offering her love to the bitter end. God had permitted Mother Mary Angelica to stay until the worst was over—for the Church and for her community. For all of us.

Rita Rizzo finally heard her Spouse say "come" on Easter, no less. Her end came like everything else in Mother's life—with pain and impeccable timing.

On March 16, 2016, one of her caretakers noticed that Mother Angelica's right leg was discolored and swollen, including her toes. X-rays revealed a broken hip. Her physicians conjectured that the heavy use of steroids in decades past and the inactivity had "washed out the bones" and weakened them. From the expression on Mother's face, the pain must have been excruciating.

In the ensuing days, palliative medication was administered and her vitals were closely monitored. Even as the swelling subsided, her sparrow-like leg began to contort horribly. By March 25, Good Friday, Mother Angelica was crying out, bleating with every breath. An attending physician upon seeing her whispered, "She is definitely in her agony." From Angelica's symptoms, the doctor believed she had experienced a "heart trauma." Morphine was dispensed.

"Mother suffered more than anyone should have to suffer," one of her caretakers, Cindy Westbrook, told me. "And she did so gloriously."

Good Friday into Holy Saturday, Angelica struggled for breath, her face a mask of torment. With great effort she accepted a tiny piece of the Eucharist on Saturday morning, though swallowing was increasingly difficult. She seemed to be choking. "She's turning purple. We're losing her," Sister Gabriel screamed, running into the hall. Then as she had so many times before, Mother suddenly rallied and her vitals spiked up.

By Easter Sunday, the day the Church commemorates Jesus's triumph over death, Mother's condition had worsened. The nuns gathered around her bedside and the caretakers were called to say their good-byes. By 4:50 PM, Angelica gasped for air. A desperate Sister Gabriel assumed a position near Mother's head, attempting to stall the inevitable. "Mother? Mother? It's me, Gabriel, honey. Mother!!"

Mother Angelica drew one last breath, her lips moving, as if attempting to say something. Then the room fell silent, except for the sobbing of her nuns.

Rita Rizzo who had lived ninety-two years in the shadow of Good Friday, returned to her Beloved on the day of His resurrection. It would be her final, glorious witness to His Divine Providence.

Mother Angelica's body was laid to rest in the crypt of Our Lady of the Angels Monastery beside her mother, Mae, and her Sisters Raphael, Joseph, Bernadette, Sharbel, and others.

She once wrote: "All the trials, sufferings, heartaches, and disappointments will seem as nothing compared to the glory Your sufferings merited for me. . . . With you, dear Jesus, I will roam freely in the love of the spirit forever and ever." Mother's spirit is finally free.

Even now she continues to make spiritual children of strangers and draw new souls to her Lord. Somewhere in a darkened hotel room, a suburban den, a hospital, or a dorm, her light shines still. In the glow of a wide-screen television or a computer monitor, beside a radio or before an open book, those in desperate straits—those confused or abandoned by life have found Mother Angelica. And inexplicably, beyond time and space, she has found them and holds them near in the present moment.

ACKNOWLEDGMENTS

THERE ARE SO many people to thank for their assistance on this final Mother Angelica book, but none more than the sisters of Our Lady of the Angels Monastery and the Poor Clares of Perpetual Adoration scattered throughout the world. Their honest and heartfelt remembrances lent my work a texture and spiritual resonance it would have lacked otherwise. My deepest thanks and affection go out to each sister mentioned in these pages, as well as those whose names are absent. My heart is filled with appreciation for the many nuns in Hanceville, Charlotte, Phoenix, San Antonio, Troyes, and even Italy who offered prayers on my behalf throughout the writing of this book. You multiplied my efforts and assisted in ways beyond imagining. For their hospitality and willingness to permit me to see Mother Angelica over many years, I will always be grateful to Mother Dolores Marie, Sister Mary Michael, Sister Genevieve Glen, and before them, Sister Mary Catherine (Mother Gabrielle Marie).

Father Joseph Mary Wolfe, Fr. Anthony Mary, Fr. Miguel Marie, Fr. Dominic Mary and the friars of the Franciscan Missionaries of the Eternal Word gifted me with their memories and candor. Thank you, gents.

Where would I be without the love of my life, Rebecca, and our children, Alexander, Lorenzo, and Mariella? They allowed me many a quiet evening in "the pit" as I labored to assemble this book. To have finished it while working on my Will Wilder/Perilous Falls middle-grade series is a testament to their understanding and love. You all teach me each day what it means to love and how deep it can run.

Special thanks to Lynda and Raymond Arroyo, my parents, who are always there; to my brother, Scott Arroyo; to Christopher Edwards, my loyal producer and friend; to Laura Ingraham, a dear sister and steadfast collaborator; to Terri Keck and Doug Keck, EWTN's president and a caring boss; to Joseph Looney and Steven Sheehy for their wise counsel; to my old friend Michael Paternostro for sticking by me; to my pal Jim Caviezel (who I know will have my back should my number ever come up!); to Umberto and Maryellen Fedeli and Lee South for their enduring friendship; and to dear Kate O'Beirne, who turned her perceptive editorial gaze upon this work and offered timely and instructive notes. Your friendship, love, and support mean the world to me.

At EWTN, for their encouragement and aid I am grateful to CEO, Michael Warsaw; my dedicated producers, James Faulkner and Cristina Kelly; my friend, Peter Gagnon; Lisa Gould, whom Mother loved dearly; Dorothy Radlicz (and the whole catalogue troupe); as well as the technical people who make us all look and sound so good.

At Image, my editor Gary Jansen shepherded this book through the editorial process with taste and aplomb at breakneck speed. Amanda O'Connor helped me out of so many binds. Megan Schumann was a supporter of this work and committed to publicizing it from the inception, and Jessica Brown has once again worked her promotional magic. I am so grateful to you all.

Loretta Barrett, my plucky agent, has been with me from the first Mother Angelica book. Her determined efforts on my behalf and those of her associates Nick Mullendore and Laura Van Wormer are such a blessing.

Finally, I send a prayer of gratitude up to dear Reverend Mother. She trusted me, from the beginning, to tell her story in full, with no sugarcoating. This work completes that story—though it goes on. Mother Angelica will always remain in my heart and be a part of the work I do. Having had the opportunity to know and work with her was a supreme honor. May her soul rest in the peace of the Lord.

Since Mother always had the last word in life, it seems only fitting to give her the last word here. During her final months of broadcasting she offered an extemporaneous prayer at the end of a live show. When I first heard it I was struck by the personal and prophetic nature of the composition, and its sense of finality. This is the prayer that concluded her program one night in 2001:

> Lord God, I am one with all the others, a sinner.
> We have not done right before you.
> And though I have warned the world, Lord, I want
>   you to give them hope.
> I want you to make them repentant.
> I want the world to serve you well.
> I want Heaven and all the angels to rejoice at all
>   the sinners that repent.
> I want you to be pleased with your creation.
> My time is up, Lord.
> Tend to my prayer.
> Amen.